The Truth
About
the Lie

DISTRIBUTED BY
CHOICE BOOKS
SALUNGA, PA. 17538
WE WELCOME YOUR RESPONSE

The Truth About the Lie

David R. Mains

Zondervan Books
Zondervan Publishing House
Grand Rapids, Michigan

Zondervan Books are published by
Zondervan Publishing House
1415 Lake Drive, S.E.
Grand Rapids, Michigan 49506

THE TRUTH ABOUT THE LIE
Copyright © 1985 by David R. Mains
Formerly titled: The Rise of the Religion of Antichristism

ISBN 0-310-34831-5

Designed and edited by Judith Markham

Printed in the United States of America.

87 88 89 90 91 92 / AH / 10 9 8 7 6 5 4 3 2 1

To Randy
and his generation
of young men and women
upon whom I pray
the Lord will pour out His Spirit

Contents

Preface

Is it brave or foolish to add one's thoughts to the existing glut of theories regarding the coming of Antichrist?

After several Chapel of the Air broadcasts in which I interviewed Donald Wildmon of the National Federation for Decency, this book first began to take form in my heart. The Lord then used this passage from Ezekiel to prod me to finish a task about which I still felt some reluctance:

> "Son of man, I have made you a watchman for the house of Israel; so hear the word I speak and give them warning from me. When I say to the wicked, 'O wicked man, you will surely die,' and you do not speak out to dissuade him from his ways, that wicked man will die for his sin, and I will hold you accountable for his blood. But if you do warn the wicked man to turn from his ways and he does not do so, he will die for his sin, but you will have saved yourself." (Ezekiel 33:7–9)

My initial hesitation was eventually overcome by a strong conviction that God had given me a message that must be delivered. I trust that what I have written maintains the urgency I feel without straying into the trap of sensationalism.

I view this book as a message of hope. Perhaps because I have prayed many years for a contemporary spiritual awakening in the North American church, I am still optimistic about that possibility. But I am also aware that a few minor adjustments will not be adequate.

We must make major shifts in our thinking, radical transformations in our attitudes, revolutionary changes in our action—and soon. That is why I have attempted to be as pragmatic as possible in suggesting concrete Life Responses in each chapter.

My prayer is that *many watchmen* will verify and amplify this message.

DAVID R. MAINS

The Truth About the Lie

1

Antichristism: What Is It?

In *Wanderings*, a history of the Jewish people, the remarkable writer Chaim Potok, author of the best-selling novels *The Chosen* and *The Promise*, states:

I write this book in Jerusalem and in certain cities of Europe and America. I write it in the bloodiest century in the history of my people; probably in the history of mankind. To be a Jew in this century is to understand fully the possibility of the end of mankind, while at the same time believing with certain faith that we will survive.[1]

The question of survival always mystifies anyone who studies the history of the Jewish people. How have they endured the enormous waves of anti-Semitism that have swept over them through the centuries? How have they survived the "crusades, the persecutions at the time of the Black Death, the Inquisition, the expulsion from Spain, the degrading ghetto centuries, the Chmielnicki rebellion, the Russian pogroms, the massacres during the First World War, and finally the Holocaust"?[2]

One reason for the survival of the Jews has been their religious life and the divine preserving action of God; another reason has been their efforts to organize vigorously on their own behalf.

An example of the latter is the B'nai B'rith, formed in 1843 to unite Jews to fight for their own best interests. Beneath its umbrella grew the Anti-Defamation League, a civil-rights organization that attempts to stop the defamation of Jewish people and to secure justice and fair treatment for all citizens. One of the organization's basic goals has been to uncover and confront anti-Semitism wherever it is found.

Anti words, like *anti-defamation* and *anti-Semitism,* are common in our culture. We have *antitrust, antihistamine, antiwar,* and a multitude of others.

Anti is a prefix meaning against or hostile to. Antiknock lubricants fight noises in your car engine. Antibiotics destroy harmful bacteria. Antilabor movements stand in opposition to unions. Antiaircraft guns are used to defend against enemy planes.

Some of these *anti* or *against* terms are neutral. No one gets excited about antifreeze. But many evoke strong emotional reactions. If you mention the antinuclear movement, you are likely to detonate strong feelings in any group. Few *anti* words, however, carry the emotional overtones associated with the term the *Antichrist.*

The specific term *antichrist* comes from the pen of the apostle John. *Antichristos* is the Greek word, and it means one who is against or hostile to Christ. A secondary meaning would be one who is a substitute christ or pseudochrist.

Another term that John uses is *antichrists*—plural rather than the singular. "You have heard that Antichrist ... is coming, even now many *antichrists* have arisen" (2 John 2:18 AMPLIFIED). Unfortunately, the simple addition of one letter immediately decreases the interest level of many Christians.

The church in North America may be as superstar-oriented as the general public. We love big names and pay little attention to the also-rans. Advertise that you are conducting an exposé on who *the* Antichrist is, and you can pack the auditorium. Warn believers that many antichrists are already among us, and the response is "Ho hum, so what else is new?"

14

Antichristism: What Is It?

But it is extremely important to understand that in his first two epistles, John is more immediately concerned with antichrists in the plural than he is with *the* Antichrist. This concern implies that we, as twentieth-century Christians, should put aside our fascination for predicting the coming of the Antichrist and begin to identify the growing danger at hand.

In 1913 the Jewish community, while wrestling the tremendous foe of anti-Semitism, wisely developed the Anti-Defamation League. If Jews had decided to overlook anti-Semitism and concentrate their activities and discussions on one powerful anti-Semite who would someday appear, what effect would they have had on the persecution that was already at hand? If the Anti-Defamation League's publications had warned only of a coming antagonist, the Jews would have been woefully unprepared for the pervasive spirit of hatred that erupted in frequent violence against them, culminating in the Holocaust of World War II.

This illustrates John's concern for his day and my concern for ours. Yes—the Antichrist is coming. *But many antichrists have already come.* Most assuredly, they are only forerunners of the future man of sin, but we cannot dismiss their power to do incredible evil.

In 2 John, the author expands upon his definition of the term *antichrist:* "Many deceivers, who do not acknowledge Jesus Christ as coming in the flesh, have gone out into the world. Any such person is the deceiver and the antichrist. Watch out that you do not lose what you have worked for" (vv. 7–8). Whether singular or plural, those who refuse to acknowledge the coming of Christ in the flesh are anti-christ—*against* Christ.

"Who is the liar? It is the man who denies that Jesus is the Christ. Such a man is the antichrist—he denies the Father and the Son. No one who denies the Son has the Father" (1 John 2:22–23).

Does John's definition mean that everyone who is not a Christian is therefore antichrist? Not necessarily. To be antichrist is to choose to stand against Christ, to be hostile to Him, to purposely hinder or oppose what Christ stands for, and to habitually side with the opposition. Although most non-Christians have said no to *following* Jesus, they often don't actively seek to defame Christ or destroy His influence. A person can be pagan (that is, without belief in the Christian God) or pursue the religions of materialism, hedonism, or humanism without being antichrist. It is imperative to keep the distinction clear.

Madalyn Murray O'Hair fits John's definition. Campaigning against Christ, she is more than merely non-Christian—she is utterly hostile to Him. In 1964 the *Saturday Evening Post* quoted her as saying, "I love a good fight. . . . I guess fighting God and God's spokesman is sort of the ultimate, isn't it?" She has become one of the nation's most outspoken atheists, founding the American Atheist Center.

In contrast, a personality like Elizabeth Taylor, whose public statements reveal a private lifestyle that could hardly be classified as Christian, is, nevertheless, not actively antichrist.

We must train ourselves to be sensitive and to discriminate between these two attitudes.

Although the B'nai B'rith was formed in 1843, racial hatred against the Jews existed long before that. It is an age-old problem. Somewhere in their history the Jewish people began to use the term *anti-Semitic* to describe their foes. Although prejudice against Jews still exists, few people today would think of themselves as anti-Semites. This indicates the progress that has been made. The term has become part of our vocabulary and, at least in the minds of most people, has a negative connotation—something wrong, something to be avoided.

It is time that we as Christians learned this same lesson and begin to recognize that it is *our* beliefs and *our* values and *our* way of life that are under attack. We need to use a new terminology. Along with such familiar modern terms as antiballistic missile, anti-imperialism, antimatter, antiseptic,

16

and anticommunist, reality demands that we add a new word to our present vocabulary—*antichristism.*

Antichristism. The term is strong, but we need powerful new ways of communicating our legitimate concern.

On an NBC television special "Celebrity," the leading character, a clergyman named Thomas Jeremiah Luther, is a rapist, a liar, a swindler, a thief, an extortionist, and a murderer. On the CBS program "After Mash" a fight breaks out after an argument between a husband and wife over religion—they represent Catholic and Baptist points of view, which are both portrayed as narrow-minded and hypocritical. On the ABC program "Hotel" a priest and a married woman commit adultery. He decides it has been a maturing experience and leaves the priesthood, while she feels the affair has made her a better wife.[3] When, one after another, such examples are cited, we begin to suspect that there is an attitude in the media that is dishonestly reinforcing negative stereotypes about Christians.

Donald Wildmon, executive director of the National Federation for Decency, states: "In seven years of monitoring television, I have not seen one program, cast in a modern day setting, in which one person depicted as a Christian was shown as a warm, compassionate, intelligent person."

I'm not opposed to drama or humor or art or literature or the real-life situations that these forms so adequately present. But when Christians are regularly shown as wimpy, lackluster, two-faced, and mindless, with none of the courage or beauty or goodness or intellect that we know the church represents, I say there is a bias that needs to be called to account. And the accusing term to use is *antichristism.*

It is time that we make it clear that the public abuse of the name Christians prize most dearly, Jesus Christ, offends us. The word *profanity* is no longer strong enough. We need to start saying, "This is *antichristism.*"

Most Americans recognize that racism is evil. They recognize it because blacks have paid the price to make this clear. Sexism is no longer as prevalent as it once was because women have protested. It is past time for the church and its people to blow the whistle on intolerance based on prejudice against our Lord and His cause.

Just as blacks have found certain epithets derogatory and have responded with the word *racism,* so Christians must deplore unfair and deprecating barbs regularly aimed our way. Because I believe in creation, does that mean I am an ultraconservative? Is it logical that those opposing my view are always moderate or better informed? I vehemently oppose this misrepresentation of facts. It is *antichristism.*

While pastoring in the inner city of Chicago during the sixties and seventies, I watched the emerging "black is beautiful" era. Members of our interracial staff and interracial congregation would travel on Saturday mornings to the south side of the city to attend Operation Push meetings. Many times we heard Jesse Jackson begin the chant that did so much to raise the consciousness of blacks.

"I may be poor . . ." Jesse would begin.
"I may be poor . . ." the people would respond.
"I may be on welfare . . ."
"I may be on welfare . . ."
"But I am . . ."
"I am . . ."
"God's child . . ."
"God's child . . ."
"I may be black . . ."
"I may be black . . ."
"But I'm beautiful . . ."
"I'm beautiful . . ."

Those were good words for both blacks and whites to hear and to repeat.

In those days it seemed as though every time I turned around my colleagues and associates were accusing me of hidden racism. But with their repeated challenges, I learned that many words I used every day were often unconsciously loaded with racist content. I discovered that there was such a thing as private racism and corporate racism. And I had to look deep into my own soul to find the hidden intentions; I had to distinguish where my accusers were correct and where I was innocent.

Racism in any man's or woman's heart decreases his or her own humanity. I am thankful that I was forced to face my own private racism and to learn a little bit about the pain of black people. I learned not only to be far more circumspect in what I said and did but also in what I thought. It was a good lesson for me.

It will also be good for everyone, Christians and non-Christians, when the accusation of antichristism begins to be understood.

Become familiar with the term. Dare to use it. Explain it in the context of anti-Semitism or racism or sexism. And pray that the day will come soon when the pressure is great enough that the general public will view antichristism as something to be abhorred.

However, also heed this important note of caution: If the word *antichristism* is to become effective on the lips of Christians, we must discipline ourselves to use the term with discrimination. If categorizing specific acts as antichristism requires caution, even more discretion must be used when pointing the finger at a given person as actually *being* antichrist.

Don't misunderstand. I'm not vacillating—now saying there are no antichrists currently among us. That would be unbiblical. Christ warned us about false prophets and false christs. But I am pleading for clear heads on this issue rather than for people to adopt the term *antichristism* and run wild with it.

After airing a three-week series of broadcasts on this topic, a listener called the Chapel of the Air office to tell us that an acquaintance of hers had been called antichrist by her husband because of her study of health foods and natural nutrition. This kind of misapplication of the term is exactly what I am warning against, and it will, in the long run, result in diluting its powerful meaning.

To review: To be truly antichrist is to stand against or be hostile to Christ. The Amplified version of 1 John 4:3 catches this strong flavor:

> And every Spirit which does not acknowledge and confess that Jesus Christ has come in the flesh [but would annul, destroy, sever, disunite Him] is not of God—does not proceed from Him. This [non-confession] is the [spirit] of Antichrist, [of] which you heard that it was coming, and now it is already in the world.

I believe the time has come for Christians to actually identify individuals who in word and deed represent antichristism. This is no different than blacks declaring, "It's in our best interest to begin calling that hatchet-swinging Lester Maddox a racist." Nor is it different than women labeling Hugh Hefner's *Playboy* philosophy as sexist.

It is important for Christians to be aware of the current presence of antichrists. It is not important right now that Christians know who *the* Antichrist is, but again, it *is* extremely important for Christians to be aware of the current presence of antichrists.

To initiate this process, I will identify four people I believe qualify as antichrist. Then I'll suggest a number of areas that should produce profitable discussion regarding other candidates for this category. My desire, of course, is for you to actively explore this topic further.

Why? To drive home the truth of what John writes; to adjust your present focus from the Antichrist (singular) to antichrists (plural); to give you a more accurate assessment of the day in which we live; and to encourage you to be sensitive—but bold—in the process of identification that I am recommending.

To begin by repeating a name already mentioned, I think it fair to classify Madalyn Murray O'Hair, head of the American Atheist Center, as antichrist. She is hostile to and against Christ as He is presented in Scripture. Whether one believes Ms. O'Hair to be gracious or obnoxious, intelligent or stupid, attractive or repulsive, is not the issue. The point is that she is antichrist. Ms. O'Hair herself would say so.

A second illustration is *Hustler* magazine publisher Larry Flynt. Once there were rumors that he had been converted and that he credited Ruth Carter Stapleton with helping him to become a born-again Christian. Left for dead five years ago on the dusty pavement of Lawrenceville, Georgia, Flynt barely survived two high-powered rifle shots fired from close range by an unknown attacker. Now a paraplegic, he admits, "I have no zest for life anymore. I came out of this ordeal an atheist."[4]

Beyond what believers see as the sexual perversions of his thirty-million-dollar-a-year publishing industry (he will soon begin producing porno videotapes; the first will feature an eighteen-year-old medically certified virgin who will be deflowered in front of the cameras), Flynt now personally manifests an aggressively hostile attitude toward Christ and the church. News reports indicate that he has turned over his business holdings to the American Atheist Center.

Naming people like O'Hair and Flynt hardly borders on the sensational. Their own words have indicted them many times. What is unusual is that I'm identifying them with a new term, one I hope will startle God's people who need to realize that *antichristism* is not just for the future.

Sun Myung Moon of the Unification Church is a third name. Unlike the other people on my list, Moon would disagree with my classification of him. "My mission," says Moon, "is to try to unite all Christians into one family before the Lord returns."[5] As a goal, it is commendable; unfortunately, the small print in Moon's spiritual contract is upsetting.

In his book *Those Curious New Cults*, William Petersen writes, "According to Moon, it is not really Jesus who will return, but rather the same messianic spirit that manifested itself in Jesus Christ will come to earth."[6]

To Moonies Jesus was a perfect man, but He wasn't God. Further, Christ failed in His mission because He was prevented from marrying a perfect woman and fathering perfect children. Tragically, Christ was crucified before this was possible.[7]

Judging from such beliefs, I suspect that Moon is using Christ more than he is serving Him. Otherwise, why would Moon's literature claim that he has been worshiped by Jesus? I believe Sun Myung Moon is another antichrist.

I offer one last example—this one from the world of secular hard-rock music. I admit to knowing very little about rock music, but I do know that many who perform it openly make direct references to the Antichrist and Satan and flaunt lifestyles that are the antithesis of following Christ.

The first album cover of the popular group Black Sabbath, whose original lead singer was Ozzie Osbourne, pictured the cross of Christ upside down. "Sabbath Bloody Sabbath," a later album, showed a nude satanic ritual with 666 stamped across the front. Replacement lead singer, Ronnie James Dio, encourages audiences to make the devil's salute used by practitioners of black magic (index and small finger extended), and as those in the audience do so, a cross bursts into flame on stage.[8]

I don't know whether Black Sabbath is a twisted public-relations hoax or a group of genuine Satan worshipers, but I believe that the apostle John's warning bears repeating: "As you have heard that the antichrist is coming, even now many antichrists have come. This is how we know it is the last hour" (1 John 2:18).

It is essential that this generation of believers reclaim an important biblical concept: the urgent need to be aware of the presence of antichrists in all generations, including our own. Just as Jewish people have built a line of defense by labeling anti-Semitism, and just as American blacks have formed protective coalitions by identifying racism, so Christians must begin to grow in their awareness of those people and institutions that are antichristian—that practice the religion of antichrist.

Life Response Section

Building Mental Awareness

Train yourself to identify personalities who fit the category of antichrist.

With a little thought most believers can identify at least a dozen such antichrists, but this will not come about without deliberate discussion.

Again, we must be careful whom we name. Whether someone is controversial or greedy or foul-minded is not the question. The question is: Is this person actually hostile to our Lord?

What world leaders would be antichrist? Some obvious answers would include government figures in the communist block. Certain dictators in third-world countries might qualify. What about a religious leader like Iran's Ayatollah Khomeini?

Take a close look at the religious world, not just at the cults or the non-Christian faiths. Here you may have to wade through difficult mental waters. For instance, what do you decide about a Protestant clergyman who denies the deity of Christ but believes that Christ was a powerful positive example and who works for the good of his church in the world?

Discovering those who are truly antichrists in this world is not always a simple process, and there will be times when we will want to suspend judgment.

What about writers and publishing companies? Do any rank as antichrists?

What about the world of education—academia?

The world of business—executives and middle-level management, financiers?

What about those involved in the arts? Playwrights, actors, artists? Or the entertainment world of singers and comedians?

What about the world of psychological counselors—psychiatrists, psychologists, new theorists, newspaper columnists who dispense advice?

23

The list of categories seems endless, but it indicates that antichristism can invade every area of life. Thus, we need to evaluate all of life.

According to the networks, homosexuals are the most effective and well-organized pressure group when it comes to lobbying the television industry. A study in the *Journal of Communication* reported that there is evidence that the networks consult regularly with the Gay Media Task Force on projects they are considering and solicit substantial input in writing and producing programs.[9]

Can the church continue to ignore its own best interests—can we ignore our stance on behalf of our Lord? We must be a church that is informed but careful; aggressive but loving, active, and compelling. Only when we are mentally aware of the spirit of antichrists can we be stimulated to lobby effectively to restore the influence of Christ in our culture.

Check It Out

To be antichrist is to choose to stand against or to be hostile to Christ, to purposely hinder or oppose what Christ stands for, as illustrated by the following example from the life of William Murray, son of Madalyn Murray O'Hair.

We walked down the long hall in silence, following the signs pointing to the school office. The doors to the classrooms stood open. As we passed one class we saw the students standing with their hands over their hearts, reciting the pledge of allegiance to the flag. My mother's face reddened. "Do they do this every day or is this something special?" she demanded.

"Every day."

She stopped dead in front of another open classroom door. Mother's eyes widened. The students were standing beside their desks with their heads bowed, reciting the Lord's Prayer. "Why in h___ didn't you tell me about this?" she spat in a hoarse whisper.

In moments we found the counselor's office, and as we entered, a young, slender man looked at us expectantly. "Hello, may I help you?" he asked pleasantly.

"You sure can, but first I want to know why those kids are praying." Mother shouted, advancing to within inches of his desk. "Why are they doing that? It's un-American and unconstitutional!"

The man swallowed. "I, uhh, well . . . Is your son a student here?" he asked.

"No," she answered. "But he will be starting today. I'm an atheist, and I don't want him taught any g___ prayers."

"Look, Mrs.—uhh, what is your name?"

"Murray—Madalyn Murray."

"Look, Mrs. Murray, nobody's ever complained about this before that I know of." He paused, searching for more ammunition. "Besides, even those who aren't very religious still think this sort of thing helps improve the tone of the school day . . ."

"Nonsense! That's just a bunch of g___ nonsense, and you know it!"

"Hey, I don't want to fight with you about this. Nothing you or I do here this morning is going to change anything. Besides, let me tell you this. There were prayers in the schools of this city before there was a United States of America. If our forefathers had wanted us to stop the practice, they would have told us that when they formed the government. Now, shall we enroll your son?"

During the drive home, Mother questioned me more about the prayers and Bible reading. When I told her I had been participating in these for years at school, she cursed me roundly, accusing me of being stupid and brainless like all men. We were almost back to the row house on Winford Road when an idea interrupted her criticism of me. "Hey, I know what we can do!" Mother said, her mood brightening.

"Tomorrow morning, I want you to start keeping a log of what happens during the school day. Make special notes on any activities that smack of religion in any form: prayer, Bible reading, songs. You know why, don't you?"

"No, Mom, I don't really. The guy said the majority wants . . ."

"You stupid fool!" she said, slapping me hard across the face. "Don't you understand what is going on yet?" Her face was flushed again. "Listen, kid, the United States of America is nothing more than a fascist slave labor camp run by a handful of Jew bankers in New York City. They trick you into believing you're free with those phony rigged elections. Just because we can run around the street free doesn't mean we are really free."

26

Antichristism: What Is It?

I sighed. *Why do I have to listen to this garbage over and over?* I thought.

"The only way true freedom can be achieved is through the new socialist man—an entire race that lives for the state. Only when all men know the truth of their animal sameness will we have true freedom. Russia is close but not close enough, or they would have let us in. The CIA probably passed bad information on us."

We halted at a red light, but Mother didn't stop talking.

"Well, if they'll keep us from going to Russia where there is some freedom, we'll just have to change America. I'll make sure you never say another prayer in that school!"

William Murray, *My Life Without God* (Nashville Tenn.: Thomas Nelson, 1982).

The following newspaper article, headlined from AP Scranton, Pennsylvania, shows the kind of pressure even the general public can effect when offended by that which is offensive to Christians.

The latest issue of Hustler magazine has been removed from most local newsstands, the result of a one-man crusade by the city's deputy police chief who is upset with a feature using naked women to illustrate Easter scenes.

"It's just a spontaneous thing that happened," Deputy Chief Frank Karam said. "It infuriated me when I saw it. It's an insult and a degradation."

The magazine carries a cover photo of a nude woman on a plexiglass crucifix. Inside, a photo essay features naked models acting out various biblical scenes associated with Easter.

Karam, who said he launched the crusade Friday as a private citizen and not deputy chief, said he has persuaded most newsstand operators to take the issue off the racks.

He also persuaded a major regional magazine distributer, Anthracite News Co. of Trenton, N.J., to collect all unsold issues from its 356 outlets in northeastern Pennsylvania.

An Anthracite spokesman agreed that Christians could find the magazine's cover offensive. The remaining copies of the magazine, which has been on sale for several weeks, will be pulled and shredded, he said.

Not everyone looks at Karam's campaign favorably. Attorney Jan Kuha, a local lawyer with the American Civil Liberties Union, said Karam's efforts bring up questions of freedom of speech and his group will consider challenging the deputy chief.

The threat failed to faze Karam.

"I know all about the Constitution," Karam said, "but I have rights as a police officer and a private citizen to make my feelings known.

"I acted in good faith. I acted as an outraged citizen. Let them do whatever they want."

Bishop James C. Timlin of the Diocese of Scranton issued a statement Friday condemning the magazine for relating "the crudest pornographic material to the holiest mysteries of the Christian religion, namely, the death of our Lord on the cross and the institution of the Holy Eucharist."

Karam said he first noticed the magazine's cover Friday, when he was browsing at Frank's News Stand in downtown Scranton. When he returned to his office, he called the owner and complained.

Jerry Frank, who operates Frank's, said he didn't find the cover offensive, but he agreed to take Hustler off the shelves.

Sid Markowitz of Scranton's Markowitz Brothers Tobacco and News Stand said he never put the May issue on the shelves.

"It's in bad taste," Markowitz said. "I never saw anything like it before."

28

Antichristism: What Is It?

Antichristism can invade every area of life, as illustrated by this comment on *The Religiosity of the Mental Health Professional.*

Perry London has written that "every aspect of psychotherapy presupposes some implicit moral doctrine" and that psychotherapists constitute a "secular priesthood" that covertly supports to establish its own moral code or standards of living. Similar and more recent theses on the substitution of psychology or psychotherapy for religion have been presented by Reiff, Lowe, Lasch, Becker, Kung and Vitz.

As described by Bergin, at least four studies have documented differences between the values of the therapists and their clients. Lillienfeld found large differences between the values of the therapists they studied and their mostly Roman Catholic clients; the discrepancies were largest concerning sex, aggression and authority with the patients far more conservative than the therapists. Vaughn found similar results to Lillienfeld, while Henry, Sims and Spray in their studies of several thousand mental health professionals in New York, Chicago and Los Angeles, found the values of the therapists to be far more religiously liberal compared with the population. Lastly Ragan et al. reporting on a random sample of the American Psychological Association found that 50% believed in God. This figure compared with the 94% of the U.S. population that believed in God, some 44% less.

In more direct studies assessing the religiosity of the therapists of which there again are few, Marx and Spray found that 28.2% of the therapists turned away from the religion of their parents, becoming either non-religious, agnostic or atheistic. I have already mentioned the findings from the American Psychological Association concerning their lack of theistic belief. Findings from the American Psychiatric Association are quite similar with 57% of those sampled being either atheistic or agnostic.

29

At this time we know little of the religious or non-religious interaction of therapists and their clients. Neither do we know about the mental health use of the large national sector of the very religious. One would expect that the religion (or lack of it) of the therapist might be quite important to these and could either retard or potentiate them to get mental health services when they needed them.

Study on Including Religious Variables As Social Support Measures, from Dave Larson, psychiatrist, serving on the Family Research Council, To HSCA Steering Committee, Department of Health and Human Services, March 30, 1984.

2

Monitoring the Media

John M. Perkins, one of the most significant Christian leaders in our nation today, grew up in Mississippi amid desperate poverty and racial persecution. The son of a black sharecropper, Perkins fled to California when he was seventeen in the wake of his older brother's murder at the hands of a town marshal. In 1960, after his conversion to Christ, he returned to his boyhood home to take part in the civil-rights movement and eventually established the Voice of Calvary Ministries in Jackson, which has become a national and worldwide prototype for Christian development. In his book, *With Justice for All,* John Perkins writes,

> The government cutback of social programs offers the church a golden opportunity as never before. For far too long we have neglected our scriptural responsibility to the poor with the excuse that "that's the government's job." We should never expect the government to provide for the needs of the poor without the Christian's active involvement. The only institution in America with the human resources adequate to meet the needs of the poor is the church. But racism and misguided patriotism have blinded the church to this great mission opportunity.[1]

Men and women like John Perkins who have suffered from prejudice know that racism in this country goes far beyond such obvious examples as the Ku Klux Klan. Even if one hundred of the most influential racists in the country suddenly had a change of heart, it would hardly eliminate this deep-rooted problem. The practice of racial discrimination not only permeates our society, but it is deeply rooted in the church. This makes it imperative that we watch for racism and denounce it and challenge it when we see it. Some improvement has been made because brave men and women did just that. But only by consistent vigilance will the eradication of this blight be achieved.

Just as racial prejudice transcends individuals to become a spirit permeating society, so antichristism stretches far beyond the coming Antichrist and the antichrists presently among us.

In his day the apostle John referred to the "spirit" of antichrist as a pervasive presence. "Dear friends," he warned, "do not believe every spirit, but test the spirits to see whether they are from God" (1 John 4:1).

A spirit does not need a body to have influence. It can take the form of a concept, an idea so large that it does not make its home in the human mind but invites the person to step into it and abide within it.

Although this spirit of antichrist is often embodied in people, we must understand that we are dealing with something beyond flesh and blood. I have no evidence of a national or international antichrist collusion, but I do not doubt that such a conspiracy exists in Satan's realm. The top item on the agenda of his dark spiritual world is the discrediting of Jesus Christ and His kingdom.

As part of his means for achieving this goal, I believe Satan is using the spirit of antichrist to gain control of the all-important communications field in our culture, and he is using human minds to communicate his insidious philosophy. Research data compiled in the recent series of Lichter/Rothman reports underscores my concern.[2]

In one study, for example, 104 people representing the cream of television's creative community were interviewed. The introduction to the report explains,

The sample includes 15 presidents of independent production companies, 18 executive producers, 43 additional producers, 26 of whom are also writers, and 10 network vice presidents responsible for program development and selection. Among those surveyed are some of the most experienced and respected members of the craft. Many have been honored with Emmy Awards, and a few are household names. Most important, this group has had a major role in shaping the shows whose themes and stars have become staples of our popular culture.

One sample finding reports that 93 percent of this influential group "seldom or never attend religious services." This doesn't mean, of course, that over nine out of ten of these professional influencers are hostile to Christ or are antichrist. But other statistics help us assess the mindset of television's creative community in regard to faith and issues of morality. Asked to list ten groups as to *perceived* influence, they put religion seventh—behind (in order) media, business, government agencies, unions, military, and consumer rights; but in reranking their *preferred* order of influences for the ten, television's elite ranked religion number nine, ahead of only the military and now trailing intellectuals, blacks, and feminists. That's the order of influence the television people would prefer.

In response to the statement, "A woman has the right to decide on abortion," 91 percent of those polled strongly agreed, 6 percent more agreed (that's 97 percent), 1 percent disagreed, and 2 percent strongly disagreed. Four out of five—80 percent—said homosexuality is not wrong; another 51 percent refused to say adultery was wrong. Of the rest, 32 percent said it is wrong, but they didn't have strong feelings on the matter. When asked whether television is too critical of traditional values, 88 percent of the writer/producers interviewed said no. A similar study among the news elite resulted in an almost identical profile, while a survey given to movie makers revealed even more extreme views on all these issues.

While I believe it is fair to conclude from these figures that there is a vast difference between the mindset of this creative community and the standards of the church of Jesus Christ, my concern is more than a disagreement over moral issues. The research also makes clear that these media leaders, by a five-to-one ratio, view the promotion of social reform as part of their role. In other words, they believe in advocating their beliefs in their work. This research reveals that news and entertainment people *are* out to reshape our society.

In *A Time for Anger: The Myth of Neutrality,* Franky Schaeffer includes an example of this disposition of the news organization to move from reporting to reorienting society:

> An instance of this occurred during the *Whatever Happened to the Human Race?* seminar at Madison Square Garden in New York City.
>
> Inside the hall we had approximately one thousand people who were spending two days watching a serious film and hearing lectures on the subjects of abortion, infanticide, and euthanasia. These were concerned people from all walks of life . . . who were difficult to stereotype and therefore difficult to put in the appropriate media pigeon hole of "prolife activists" (who the media prefer to characterize as senile retired nuns!).
>
> Outside the seminar hall on the sidewalk, there was a group of twelve people (I counted them) who arrived to picket the proceedings within as being "antichoice" and therefore dangerous.
>
> "Coincidentally," they arrived and unpacked their four or five well-worn "prochoice" placards at the same time as a television truck arrived from the *Village Voice,* as well as some other media persons. Their picketing lasted for the exact amount of time it took the television truck to unpack its cameras, film them for a minute or so, and for the anchor person to do her "wrap-up" (twenty seconds) on the story.

> The television cameras and the "reporter" never ven-
> tured into the auditorium, much less asked any of us, the
> organizers, what we were doing and saying, why one
> thousand people were inside talking and watching
> movies for two days. The three-minute "protest" was the
> story.[3]

Unlike many people, I don't see this as an organized
effort of the media to defame Christ and His church. Rather,
I believe it reveals the subtle, behind-the-scenes skill of the
spirit of antichrist. I am awed by this ingenious takeover of
such a powerful media tool for molding people's thinking.

Furthermore, it is working. People are being influenced
by these mind-changers. According to one report, the average American adult watches television forty-two hours a
week. If, for the sake of argument, Christian intake of secular
television is only half that much, it would still be a
whopping twenty-one hours a week—or three hours a day.

Overexposure to secular input is dangerous. We can't
spend dozens of hours each week viewing programs and
listening to people who view Christ as irrelevant to life
without subconsciously buying into their philosophy.

For example, many Christians today see beauty as
exclusively physical. But is it? Would Christ agree that
Christy Brinkley or Joan Collins are beautiful women? What
about the inward qualities of beauty emphasized in Scripture?

What about success? Just try defining success by the
standards set in films or on the top television shows. I
guarantee it won't come anywhere close to Christ's
definition of the word.

So be careful. We live in a media culture that invites us
to make pleasure our ultimate goal, to seek satisfaction for all
human desires, to *overindulge.*

> With each overindulgence, the level of physical and emotional expectation gradually rises so that an increasingly greater thrill is required to satisfy the urge. Eventually, the thrill begins to diminish but the hunger for stimulation is ever present, now stronger than ever. Without finding full satisfaction, the hunger need settles into the monotony of filling and emptying. One begins by seeking pleasures to fill his boredom and ends by being bored with his pleasures. As Shakespeare said, "If all the years were playing holidays, to sport would be as tedious as to work."[4]

Yes, the spirit of antichrist is insidious; it is devious and wily, operating in a manner more dangerous than seems apparent.

Suppose that you carefully monitor, as a family, what television shows you watch. Together, you decide that viewing the Olympics is a healthy and inspiring choice. Then you're caught by a surprise commercial for a new mini-series that paints open sin as extremely attractive (which it is, if you think only in terms of immediate gratification). Dad, at that point do you take the time to explain this allure to your junior-high-age son sitting beside you? Or do you expect him to figure out on his own that this is an attempt by the spirit of antichrist to ensnare young men like himself? What about the seemingly innocent commercial break advertising a soft drink with suggestive, erotic shots and dialogue?

So what are we to do? Cut ourselves off from everything except the Sunday-school take-home paper?

No. What I'm saying is that the powerful media influence on our society makes it imperative that Christians know how to detect and defeat the *spirit* of antichrist. It is not a time to be naive. For it is not just specific evil people we must guard against; it is something much more pervasive. We must develop a mental radiation shield to ward off the malignant lies that continue to bombard us and permeate our corporate society.

That is why I've trained myself to hear the word *secular* as also meaning antichrist, since, for the most part, that's what it is. The dictionary defines secularism as "a system of doctrines and practices that rejects any form of religious faith and worship." Therefore, the adjective "secular," as in secular music, secular education, or secular media, defines an attitude or a mindset or a spirit that rejects the Son of God as someone of true importance.

Secular music is often antichrist music. Just note the implications of this quote from Allan Bloom, professor of the Committee on Social Thought at the University of Chicago, in the *Wall Street Journal:*

> Rock music caused a great evolution in the relations between parents and children. Its success was the result of an amazing cooperation among lust, art and commercial shrewdness . . .
>
> The most powerful formative influence on children between 12 and 18 is not the school, not the church, not the home, but rock music and all that goes with it. It is not an elevating but a leveling influence. The children have as their heroes banal, drug-and-sex-ridden guttersnipes who foment rebellion not only against parents but against all noble sentiments. This is the emotional nourishment they ingest in these precious years. It is the real junk food.
>
> One thing I have no difficulty teaching students today is the passage in the "Republic" where Socrates teaches that control over music is control over character and that the rhythm and the melody are more powerful than the words. They do not especially like Socrates's views on music, but they understand perfectly what he is about and the importance of the issue.[5]

The majority of secular films are antichrist, as evidenced by their use of profanity, their consistent negative portrayal of Christians—especially ministers—and their obvious rejection of the ethics that Christ taught. And doesn't secular education consistently manifest a hostile attitude toward Christ?

Secular is not a neutral word. It describes the unholy spirit that is actively at work in our world. And while we know that the powerful Holy Spirit is also active, we must become experts at spotting the lies that characterize His enemy.

Deception Can Be Beautiful

What does Satan look like? In 2 Corinthians 11:14, it says, "Satan disguises himself as an angel of light" (rsv). In 2 Thessalonians 2, Paul implies that the same deception will mark the man of sin who appears on the scene at the end of the age. By nature he is a beast, but apparently this is not how he is generally perceived. Instead, he deludes people into believing he is the great savior of the world.

His emissaries, his antichrists, frequently are attractive people. An extremely popular talk-show host, whom I personally would classify as antichrist, is articulate, witty, bright, informed, interesting, persuasive, and at times downright winsome; and he rarely misses an opportunity to denigrate the lifestyle and people of Christ.

No warning light flashes on and off—Beware of the spirit of antichrist! Beware of the spirit of antichrist!—when messages hostile to our Lord appear attractively disguised in films, magazines, books, or direct-mail advertising. For this reason, Christians must develop their own quiet signal of warning within.

For example, when *Time* magazine arrives in our home, I read it with a certain mindset I have developed. While opening its pages, I remind myself not only that it has been composed from a perspective that views Christ as irrelevant, but that occasionally its approach will even be slanted, hostile, or antichrist. I suppose that rather than do this, I could avoid all but Christian publications. And already as a family we have made radical cuts in the number of periodicals we support through our subscription dollars. But at present I find this conscious mental reminder an adequate buffer from the basic presuppositions in *Time* or other magazines and newspapers I might find it necessary to read.

There are, however, many aspects of the mass media to which I will not expose myself or my family. I have never read *Playboy*. The publication is blatantly antichrist, and therefore I will have nothing to do with it. My conclusion is based on the striking contrast between Christian faith and the *Playboy* philosophy and on my understanding that any strategy that makes obvious sin appear not only attractive but acceptable is basic to enemy tactics.

I believe that my decision about which movies to attend or to recommend must involve more than merely checking whether a film is rated G, PG, PG13, R, or X. Antichrist messages can be found in any of these categories, so I need to take more than violence or adult situations into consideration. And while national critics such as Gene Siskel and Roger Ebert can provide certain guidelines with their new-movie reviews, I know I must go far beyond the critics. I must ask, "What does this movie say about my Lord and the way of life He advocates?"

Christians must learn to exercise discernment. We can't go to a movie just because "we feel like it." We must stop the practice of turning on the television just "to see if something interesting is on." These and familiar excuses like the following open the doors to the spirit of antichrist:

"I didn't have anything better to do, so I watched it."

"The magazine was there in the waiting room so I looked at it. I'd never buy one myself, I mean . . . but face it, I was curious!"

"It came in the mail. What was I supposed to do? Run and throw it in the trash before the children saw it?"

"Come on . . . leave me alone. All the kids listen to AC/DC; it's one of the hottest groups going!"

"Everybody said it's a great book—it's been on the bestseller list for weeks."

If you don't believe me, *whisper these rationalizations to Christ. How quickly our excuses disintegrate when the Lord stands near.*

We live in a media age. All that's good, and all that's bad, and all that's in-between is available to us, often right in our own homes. Fifty years ago it was a major event when a well-known personality came to town. The mayor and council, the townspeople, and bands flocked to the train station in welcome. Now, people in the most remote places can view the famous and the infamous twenty-four hours a day.

This same media also offers incredible exposure to a great diversity of values. A child's world is no longer restricted to the influences of family, neighbors, school, and church. The red-light district is no longer bounded by certain streets; many of its attractions are now on a cable attached to hundreds of thousands of homes in neighborhoods everywhere. One need not travel to the big city to see its fabled and sometimes forbidden merchandise. Catalogs in the mailbox every week unfold these wonders in full color, their whole merchandising approach built on creating a lust for goods.

"Listen!" "Look!" "Buy!" these images say. "Clap!" "Laugh!" "Agree!" And inherent in many of these messages is a spirit that says, "Agree with us. Trust and believe in what you're being offered; for *here* is where the good life is to be found."

Preachers aren't the only ones seeking converts. If you think they are, you're dangerously naive.

In this media-crazy world, Christians must develop the intellectual capacity to discern the mindset behind anything they watch, hear, read, and see. To use the apostle John's terms, we must learn to "test the spirits." The time has come to be more perceptive, to reject the false, and hold tightly to the true whether in regard to an entertainment series, a political candidate, a favorite media talk show, a comic strip, or a best-selling author.

So you bought a book that's proven to be opposed to Christ's precepts. You don't have to finish it just because you paid for it. Throw it in the garbage—all $25 worth. Next time you'll be more careful.

Cancel that magazine subscription when careful thought reveals that its content consistently runs counter to the higher values of the kingdom, whether the subject is travel, fashion, news, sports, or homemaking.

If you're the one who walks into the room and without thinking goes to the television set just to see what's on, change your habits. Learn to be selective. Predetermine your viewing by checking television content with a guide; vow to spend only so much time with secular media input. When you master this tough lesson, maybe there's a chance your children will also.

When going to the theater, be willing to get up and walk out if you find your beliefs being compromised.

Get used to telling yourself, "I won't dwell on that thought—it's evil. I refuse to give my attention to a lying spirit!"

In this world's critical setting, a setting preparing for the appearances of Christ and Antichrist, don't remain uncritical. Learn to ask, "What is really being said here? Is it consistent with my Christian beliefs—or is it antichristian? Does it affirm what is at the very core of who I am? What parts must I as a Christian then reject? As a follower of Jesus Christ, do I oppose the value system this author (or film maker or newscaster or entertainer) states or implies?"

I'm not suggesting there's a demon behind every best seller, every marquee, or every magazine article. Nor am I attempting to create a new list of don'ts. I'm only warning that we are living on a battlefield, and the warfare is fierce;

the weapons deadly. If we remain indifferent to this battle of spiritual worlds in progress, we could be wounded.

In Daniel's day, King Nebuchadnezzar erected an image of gold and commanded all his subjects to fall down and worship it. Anyone who did not obey would be executed. Three of God's people, Shadrach, Meshach, and Abednego, refused to worship the king's image. Despite sentence of death, they replied, "We will not serve your gods."

Today, the call to worship the image is being sounded throughout the media, and the image is the beast of antichrist! Constant vigilance is necessary if we are to detect and defeat this foul spirit. We, too, must refuse to bend the knee. We, too, must say boldly, "We will not serve your gods."

Life Response Section

Draw Your Own Conclusions

Examine your answers to each of the following categories. Do they reflect Christian values, are they neutral, do they give evidence of the spirit of antichrist, or are they blatantly antichrist? You will have to draw your own conclusions because there are so many variables. While the conclusions themselves are important, the exercise of forcing yourself to consider these everyday influencers may actually be more important if it encourages you to practice discernment and monitor the media.

	Christian	Neutral	Reflects Spirit of Antichrist	Blatantly Antichrist
1. News magazine most often read				
2. Favorite media talk show (non-religious)				
3. Advertiser whose direct mail I normally examine				
4. Entertainment series watched regularly on television				
5. Non-religious cause with which I identify				
6. Favorite actor or actress				
7. Newspaper most often read				

	Christian	Neutral	Reflects Spirit of Antichrist	Blatantly Antichrist
8. Popular music group or artist I like				
9. Favorite comic strip				
10. A respected political personality				
11. Company with commercials I enjoy				
12. An admired sports figure				
13. Sports, home, or fashion magazine read often				
14. Most listened to radio or television news show				
15. A favorite non-religious writer				

Check It Out

What we watch does affect us, whether we realize it or not.

Dr. Thomas Mulholland and Dr. Eric Peper of San Francisco State University conducted an experiment on the effect of television on the brain wave patterns of children.

When awake and receiving external stimuli, one's mind operates at one of two brain wave frequencies called Alpha and Beta. Alpha waves indicate that the motor of the mind is in neutral. Beta waves mean that the mind is active, thinking. When awake the mind can slip in and out of either one of these states with comparative ease.

Alpha, slow brain-wave pattern, indicates diminished mental activity; rational thinking and discernment are inoperative or semifunctional at best. The mind is *highly receptive,* but equally passive. Sensory stimuli are encoded but not analyzed; incoming information generally has no verbal labels attached to it nor value judgments made of it.

Beta, active brain-wave pattern, indicates we are in charge of our thoughts, that we are purposefully gathering information and we are in control of what is being encoded. We attach labels to the inflow of information and react to it with value judgments.

Doctors Mulholland and Peper hypothesized that children watching their favorite television shows would have predominantly Beta wave patterns. Contrary to this hypothesis, the electroencephalograph readings revealed that the brains of these children stayed almost totally in Alpha. "They just sat back. They stayed almost totally in alpha . . . not reacting, not orienting, not focusing, just spaced out."

Since this experiment, other research reports similar results in adults. The mind begins to respond to the medium, to the flickering light, the constant motion, the lack of demand for eye movement; rather than to the information, the drama or content. Television sets its own pace—a pace too rapid for left hemisphere analysis. The mind begins to shut down to alpha wave patterns—a passive but receptive mental attitude. Since the images cannot be controlled or rejected as one watches but are inside the mind before judged as acceptable, the viewer merely surrenders to them!

Dr. Peper states the danger of this Alpha-level non-critical assimilation even more forcefully:

The horror of television is that the information goes in, but we don't react to it. It goes directly into our memory pool—later we react to it but we don't know what we're reacting to. We have trained ourselves not to react, but later on we do things without knowing why, or even where the impulses come from.

Richard L. Fredericks, "Television and the Christian Family," Andrews University School of Graduate Studies, Winter, 1981. He uses material from Jerry Mander, *Four Arguments for the Elimination of Television* (New York: William Morrow and Co., 1978), 200, 209–210.

We live in a media age, with all that's good, and all that's bad, and all that's in-between available right in our own homes.

Behavior therapists tell us that values can be quickly extinguished through a method known as systematic desensitization. "Systematic desensitization" writes Dr. Joseph Wolpe, "is most effective when done with images . . . in a non-threatening environment. . . . This technique is effective in stripping people of their feelings by whittling away at emotions until a person can remain relaxed, undisturbed and unmoved even as he watches scenes that had originally occasioned his gravest concern, acutest distress, most painful anxiety.

"Those who practice this technique claim that the emotionless state it brings about becomes generalized so that when a person trained in imaginal desensitization comes upon scenes in real life that are the same or similar to those he has seen over and over again in imaginary dramas he can even then remain detached and unmoved by them."

The precise six-step process used by a behavior modification therapist to extinguish aversion and replace it with acceptance:

1. The person views familiar images in a comfortable, non-threatening situation. He is completely relaxed. No emotional arousal is noted.

2. Certain images or scenes known to arouse emotional reactions are introduced.

3. The scene shifts or viewing is interrupted. Viewer's arousal is not allowed time to react.

4. Viewer is given a respite period of approximately one minute during which he resumes a relaxed mental and physical state. This is facilitated by eating or drinking.

5. As the viewer's emotions subside, viewing of non-threatening images has resumed. Subject is completely relaxed. No strong feelings are noted.

6. The cycle is repeated.

Therapists who use systematic desensitization claim that it usually only requires twenty to thirty exposure sessions to alter a person's feelings from acceptance to rejection, or rejection to acceptance. The presentations are simple and artistically unembellished.

Television has enjoyed a luxury no behavior modification therapist ever dreamed of. It has been allowed to work in its subject's most relaxed, natural and non-threatening environment—his home. In addition, there were no strangers present to put the viewer on guard. But most of all television has been allowed to rehearse its basic collection of limited themes over and over again—not thirty, but thousands of times; not in a weekly session but daily.

Its format has adhered to the six-step cycle of desensitization religiously, using the swiftness of technical shifts and the interjection of commercials to refine the art of emotional arousal and diffusion to new heights.

Americans, say Goldsen, have the dubious distinction of being the first culture to passively submit themselves and their children to a coast-to-coast and lifelong process of mass behavior modification via an electronic hookup in their own homes.

Richard L. Fredericks, "Television and the Christian Family," Andrews University School of Graduate Studies, Winter, 1981.

3

The Danger of Selective Secularism

Like many others, I have a conviction that the return of the Lord is not far away. And although it is a delight to imagine that I might be a part of that generation of stewards who will be on duty when He makes His appearance, I am not delighted by the circumstances that are the major prompters of that conviction—my observation of the times in which we live.

Christ detailed specific world conditions that would precede His return. In such Scripture passages as the Olivet Discourse (Matthew 24) He predicted, "Nation will rise against nation, and kingdom against kingdom, and there will be famines and earthquakes in various places." Most of the conditions Jesus speaks of in the New Testament have been characteristic of every age—earthquakes, wars, the clash of the kingdoms of light and darkness, false teachers, famines, disease. If Jesus intended these to be special signs of the impending climax of history, it would seem that they should be evident in markedly increasing occurrences.

Although evil conditions have been inherent to the dilemma of mankind, there does seem to be an acceleration of evil and disaster in our age. Consider these crucial questions and observations: Is world famine being talked about more or less? Has evidence of lust and violence increased or diminished? A Harvard seismologist observes that in the last six centuries the incidence of earthquakes has gone up 2,189 percent. In this generation the Gospel is being spread around the world in unprecedented fashion.

How do you evaluate signs like widespread persecution of believers? In *By Their Blood*, journalists Jim and Marti Hefley chronicle the martyrdom of twentieth-century Christians. They quote a tape that was recorded by missionary Paul Carlson shortly before his death in which he asked his home church to pray for revival in the Congolese church. "They do not realize," he said, "that in this century more people have died for their witness for Christ than died in the early centuries, which we think of as the days of the martyrs."[1]

What about the constant talk, even on the nightly news, of the need for peace and security? What about the increased spirit of materialism and the greater abundance of scoffers? In his book *Future Shock*, Alvin Toffler writes,

> To survive, the individual must become infinitely more adaptable and capable than ever before. He must search out totally new ways to anchor himself, for all the old roots—religion, nation, community, family, or profession—are now shaking under the hurricane impact of accelerative thrust.[2]

"Understand this," says Paul to Timothy, "that in the last days there will come times of stress" (2 Timothy 3:1 RSV). One of the evidences of increased stress in our day is the toll it takes on physical well-being. The toll is so great that it has been carefully measured in terms of dollar loss by American corporate business. In 1976, premature death of employees cost American industry more than the combined profits of *Fortune*'s top five corporations—almost $20 billion. Nearly 32 million workdays and over $8 billion in wages are lost annually from heart-related diseases alone.

Hospitalizations and early death among executives cost

The Danger of Selective Secularism

an estimated 10 to 20 billion dollars. Corporations must spend over $500 million just to recruit new executives to replace those felled by heart disease.

Another cause of absenteeism and related medical costs is the problem of alcoholism, costing industry nearly $15 billion a year.[3]

In his book *Executive Health* Philip Goldberg states, "In a very real sense, we have been a Type A society, aggressive, competitive, and oriented toward achievements that can be measured in numbers like Gross National Product." According to studies on occupational stress, only one in six persons claims to be relatively free of stress, while 83 percent feel they are experiencing a great deal of stress as a result of their jobs.[4]

Paul's list of last-day conditions goes on: "For men will be lovers of self, lovers of money, arrogant, abusive, . . . unholy, inhuman." Does anyone other than this religious world-watcher sense the accuracy of Paul's words—"inhuman, . . . treacherous, reckless, . . . lovers of pleasure rather than lovers of God"(2 Timothy 3:2–3 RSV)?

FBI agent James Murphy says that children of three years old and older are being *kidnapped* for sex services. "You can order a child by height and weight," he says. "Many of these boys and girls are murdered when the porn dealers are finished so no one will be around to testify against them."[5]

Such true horrors of our society are only now coming to light. The number of reported cases of child abuse in the U.S. is rising sharply. In 1976 the American Human Association found that 413,000 cases of child abuse had been reported to state and local authorities. By 1981 the count had doubled to 851,000. In 1982 it climbed by 12 percent.[6]

These are only the reported cases. Some experts guess them to be the 'tip of the iceberg' . . . but what is known is that the cost in physical and emotional suffering, ruined lives and future crimes (studies of prison populations show that upwards of 90 percent of all inmates claim to have been abused as children) is intolerable. Even more intolerable, child abuse perpetuates itself. In a great preponderance of cases—estimates run as high as 90 percent—the abusive parent was an abused child.[7]

Scripture also tells of signs of a different nature that will presage the end of this world. These are events or conditions that have not occurred or existed before and that will unfold only as the great day of the Lord draws near. One example would be what Christ called "signs in the heavens." Another would be the present nation of İsrael.

After the Captivity of the Jews, as recorded in the Old Testament, Israel vanished from existence as a nation. Then, in our generation, despite enormous odds and incredible opposition, Israel was arduously reborn. In the history of the world, nothing like this has ever happened—a nation coming back to life after centuries of oblivion. Yet biblical prophecies indicated that that is exactly what would happen and that it would precede the coming of the Lord.

Now, narrow your focus to Jerusalem, the holy city of faith for three great monotheisms, and note Christ's words about it being "trampled on by the Gentiles until the times of the Gentiles are fulfilled. . . . When these things begin to take place, stand up and lift up your heads, because your redemption is drawing near" (Luke 21:24, 28). Jerusalem is now under Jewish domination. "Truly, I tell you," said Jesus, "this generation," as the Amplified Bible puts it "(that is, those living at that definite period of time) will not perish and pass away until *all* has taken place" (Luke 21:32).

The Danger of Selective Secularism

Preparing the Way

My expectation that Christ could soon return is accompanied by an awareness that the Antichrist's appearance must also take place at this same general time. Precisely *when* the man of sin will be revealed is not as germane as the fact that the two occurrences will not be far apart.

This is not news to believers. However, there is something that most believers seem to overlook: The Antichrist will not pop up overnight out of nowhere. There will be a preparing of the way for this pseudochrist; a favorable climate will be established for him. The Scripture teaches that the world will become even more evil at its close, much like the days of Noah.

But how can this happen? you ask. Whether they believe in Christ or not, most people don't want a rotten, evil world—not if they recognize it for that. But the enemy is as subtle and crafty today as he was in the Garden of Eden. He can make black look white and good look bad. He can deceive people into thinking that evil is really good.

One of his methods is twisting the meaning of words. Michael Braun and George Rekers write in *The Christian in an Age of Sexual Eclipse:*

> The language we use has potential not only for clear communication, but for manipulation and confusion as well. . . . When the Nixon White House tried its infamous cover-up of the Watergate scandal, the press secretary, in the early stages of the discovery that corrupt actions had occurred, flatly denied any misconduct. This was a simple lie. Later when the lies were revealed to be lies, the secretary made an announcement that his previous explanation was "inoperative." Later still, he tried to convince reporters that his previous statements had been "misspoken" . . .

53

If we, through some magical act of verbal coronation, can only give nicer names to our evil actions, then perhaps our actions won't appear as evil as they are. . . . It would be harder to convince ourselves that there is nothing wrong with *lying, dishonesty* and *deception.* If we identify these acts with their proper titles we become painfully aware that they should never be "operative." Through the magic of "redefinition," old sins become "viable alternatives". . . .

Sexual behavior today is a battlefield in which the word games are in fact war games. If someone wants to pursue an immoral sexual life, it should not be surprising that he would try to rename his actions to make them sound nicer.[8]

Permissiveness becomes "sexual freedom." Premarital relations become "trial marriages." Prostitution becomes "surrogate therapy." Homosexuality becomes an "alternate lifestyle." Abortion becomes "terminated pregnancy." Death becomes "liberty." Profanity becomes "adult language." Incidentally, in 1983 the use of profanity on television jumped by 139.1 percent! This twisting of meaning makes our evil actions more palatable and contributes to our modern moral decline.

Along with this acceleration of evil, we can anticipate a growing hostility *against* righteousness; more specifically, we can expect Antichrist and his church. Anti-forces, by definition, best generate their steam through what they are against. The force Hitler used to try and bring about his world order was an attitude *against* the Jews (anti-Semitism) rather than *for* his master race. Earlier generations of Americans found it more profitable to "prove" what blacks were not rather than demonstrating what whites were.

We must expect the enemies of Christ to take the offensive against Christians—and this is antichristism. We must anticipate the promotion of lies and half truths to cover the shambles of countless lives destroyed by the temporary joys of promiscuity, alcoholism, greed, homosexuality, gambling, and a multitude of other sins.

Consider this exchange on "Saturday Night Live" as reported in the *National Federation for Decency Journal*. It was a takeoff on a Lorne Green dog-food commercial:

> "I'm Lorne Green and this is Lucky [pointing to his dog]. Lucky is eight, that's 56 in human years. Now you might think that the most important thing in Lucky's life is exercise and a good diet of beef and meat by-products. But that's not so.
>
> "The most important thing to ol' Lucky here is his personal relationship to God. That's right—*Powerful Living* (holds up book by the same title). Now I'm sure a lot of you folks out there have heard of this new book, and I know a lot of you want to read it just like Lucky does. Of course he can't. He's a dog. That's why the folks at American Foods created Powerful Living Snacks. New crunchy, bite-sized nuggets filled with all the vitamins, minerals and faith to face tomorrow that a young dog needs. Powerful Living Snacks, from the folks that brought you Woofy Wafers. There you go, Lucky. Take, eat."[9]

The last two words were spoken slowly and distinctly leaving no doubt as to their implication. That's blasphemy!

Increasingly, Christianity is the object of scorn and ridicule. Eastern religions fare quite well in the media. In fact, the unwholesome supernatural—whether clairvoyants, psychics, the occult, witches, the realm of evil spirits— receives expanding valuable and positive coverage.

Did you know that on any given Sunday in this land, more people attend church services than the entire yearly attendance at all the major-league baseball games put together? But how much coverage is the church given in the press?

As Christians, we have been blind to what is happening. We have not seen, nor wanted to see, the sinister force at work. It is not opposed to the supernatural. What it despises is Christianity.

Preachers habitually term this spirit of our age "secular humanism." I suppose the term is partially correct, but it is also woefully inadequate. It is too neutral, too intellectual. What we're seeing is *selective secularism,* the aggressive, powerful, growing, blatant, end-time religion of the Antichrist!

If the phrase "the religion of antichrist" seems inappropriate, consider this: *Webster's New World Dictionary* defines religion as the "belief in a divine or superhuman power to be obeyed and worshiped as the ruler of the universe." If Christianity is the religion of Christ and the belief of those who worship and obey Him, isn't antichristianity the religion of those who are against Him? This religion would exclude Christ and His people from any meaningful input they might have upon the world scene; it preaches a non-morality opposed to biblical Christianity and deliberately attacks many traditional standards.

Today we are surrounded by the rise of this religion of antichristism, and we must get used to thinking in this terminology, or we will be deceived into laughing and clapping and sleeping right through its ascendency. Notice these verses from the pen of the apostle Paul:

> Don't let anyone deceive you in any way, for that day [the day of the return of our Lord] will not come until the rebellion occurs, and the man of lawlessness is revealed ... [who] will oppose and exalt himself over everything that is called God or is worshiped, so that he sets himself up in God's temple, proclaiming himself to be God (2 Thessalonians 2:3–4).

The Danger of Selective Secularism

Obviously what I am concerned about is much more than doctrinal fine points. It is an unfolding headline story that you'll never read in the *Boston Globe,* the *Chicago Tribune,* the *L.A. Times,* or the *Washington Post.* Nevertheless, the news is breaking even as we go about our daily routines.

We are seeing more than just another era of the flaunting of evil. We are witnessing the prelude to the final great battle of the superpowers. This constant encroachment on traditional Christian values—the dismembering of unborns, the demand that homosexuality be viewed as an acceptable alternative lifestyle, the wide dissemination of pornographic materials that even portray bestiality, the widespread abuse of children, and the consistent serving up of violence on our entertainment menu—this annoying tune of encroachment now has a sinister counterpoint. It is not quite as loud, but it is destined to overwhelm the present themes. If you listen closely, you'll hear it already in the music of some of the hard-rock groups. It is the naming of the Antichrist and Lucifer as the one worthy of praise, to be exalted as "sweet Satan."

Christians must be alert to the rise of the religion of antichrist as we prepare for the return of our great king. We cannot remain ignorant. Neither can *we* be an anti-force. We cannot afford to just emphasize what we are against. Our strength is in who we are.

Yes, the true king and the pretender will arrive in close proximity. Jesus said,

> But take heed to yourselves and be on your guard lest your hearts be overburdened and depressed—weighed down—with the giddiness and headache and nausea of self-indulgence, drunkenness and worldly worries and cares pertaining to (the business of) this life, and that day come upon you suddenly like a trap or a noose; . . . Keep

57

awake then and watch at all times (Luke 21:34, 36 AMPLI-
FIED).

Watch is a continual reminder throughout the New
Testament. Yet there is sometimes legitimate confusion over
what Christ meant.

First, He meant for us *to be aware of the predicted
signs,* to avoid the extremes of too little interest *and* too great
an interest. In other words, we are to be aware of what's
ahead without becoming enamored with the study of proph-
esy. Keep a healthy balance. I like the practical flavor of Paul
in 1 Thessalonians 5:4–6: "But you, brothers, are not in
darkness so that this day should surprise you like a thief. . . .
So then, let us not be like others, who are asleep, but let us
be alert and self-controlled."

Such verses lead us to the second and more important
meaning of *watch,* which is *to live in a state of preparedness.* This means that Christ wants me to conduct my life
in such a manner that if He were to come today or
tomorrow—at any moment—there would be no regret what-
soever on my part. Rather, He would find me doing, to the
best of my ability, what I know pleases Him, and I would not
have to say:

"If only I had made that relationship right."

"Oh, how I wish this sin didn't still mark who I am!"

"I'm disappointed that I didn't share my faith with
certain of my friends or family."

"I'm embarrassed that my heart is not as loyal to Him as
it was in those first days when I knew His gracious
forgiveness."

To be in constant preparedness is to conduct your life in
such a manner that all thoughts of His coming bring a
response of "May it be so Jesus. I'm ready!"

Now a point of clarification: Personally, I'm not sure it is
healthy for preachers to challenge people to make *every
decision* on the basis of whether or not Christ might come
back today or tomorrow. That tends to make Christians too

short-sighted. But what if we think in terms of the King returning within the next decade and a half—let's say by the year 2000?

Suppose I could promise you that somewhere within the next fifteen years the climactic sequence of events would culminate in our Lord's return. Would it affect the way you presently live? Would it make a difference in the way you use your time? Entertainment is a huge industry in North America today. Would it remain a priority for you? What would you see as important to share with your children? Would you invest your money differently? What voices would you heed? How significant would the study of Scripture be in your schedule? Or what if you *knew* Christ was to return within the next twenty-five to thirty years? How would this knowledge affect the way you presently live? Wrestle with these questions.

Finally, *watch* means *to carry with you this unquestioned hope*.

Throughout history and into the present day, my fellow believers have paid dearly for identifying with the true king. I "watch" in a nice studio, prepare my words in a comfortable office, and drive home each evening for dinner with a family I love. Many love us and help us in our ventures. For far too great a number, however, "watch" means another day with little to sustain them and great heartbreak to bear. Often the only joy and excitement they carry is their unquestioned hope—"Maranatha! Someday my great king comes again." For their sake, may it be soon!

My family likes the "Herman" cartoons drawn by Canadian artist Jim Unger. One of my favorites is particularly apt at this point.

Herman is struggling to carry his middle-aged wife through the door. He's straining, his beet-red face a grimace, his tie askew. The woman is huge and homely and carries a bouquet. "Herman," she says, oblivious to the fact that she has put on more than a little weight, "you were a much stronger man on our *first* honeymoon!"

After my initial chuckle, for some reason I thought of Christ and His bride. How attractive she was when young. Now obese, self-indulgent, reticent to look at herself the way she really is, she pretends *her* flaws are His. "You're not as strong as you once were! You don't sweep me off my feet like you used to. I don't find myself longing for your presence, looking forward to your return!"

Nothing is wrong with our Lord. It is His bride, the church, that must get back into condition. Hear Jesus say:

"Watch! Be aware of the predicted signs."

"Watch! Live in a state of preparedness."

"Watch! Carry in your heart this unquestioned hope, even when witnessing the rise of the religion of antichrist."

The evil pretender will not depose our true monarch. The real king will return on time, in victory, and with praise for all those who remain faithful.

Life Response Section

Initiating Personal Lifestyle Changes

What are the five most important changes you would make in your personal lifestyle if you knew Christ would return within the next ten to fifteen years? Take a moment to list them below:

1.

2.

3.

4.

5.

Now think about what we have discussed in the previous chapters. Do present conditions indicate that you should institute these changes now?

Check It Out

If Jesus intended these to be special signs of the impending climax of history, it would seem that they should be evident in markedly increasing occurrences. Take note of this item from the *Evangelical Newsletter* of 25 May 1984.

William P. Neufeld is Director of the Trend Analysis Program of the American Council of Life Insurance. The *Futurist* includes his summary article ("Forecasting Potential Crises," April) and five TAP report excerpts, which briefly describe areas of potential crisis. Neufeld points out, ". . . crises do not occur randomly or without warning. They are preceded by—and dependent upon—forces that can be identified well in advance. . . . If we heed the warning signals and act to avoid these events or to deal with the consequences, those actions will have their own implications—for our lives and for our businesses." What five potential crises are identified?

First, *the warming of the earth.* "Evidence suggests that, in the past two decades, between 40 and 50% of the carbon dioxide produced by human activity has remained in the atmosphere. Warm air is then trapped on the earth's surface, creating a warming, greenhouse effect." Second, *the water shortage.* "The United States has abundant overall water supplies but, as in the case of many other natural resources, poor management and wasteful use patterns are cutting into both supply and quality."

The third potential crisis is *the collapse of the physical infrastructure.* "This decay is pervasive, including interstate and urban roads, bridges, water and sewage systems, railroads, dams, public buildings—and probably other portions of the system, such as hardline communications networks and energy/power generation systems. . . . The estimates for rebuilding the existing U.S. infrastructure are as much as $3 trillion. . . ." Four, *the global financial crisis.* "A breakdown of the international monetary and trading system would plunge the world into prolonged depression—and such a breakdown is far from a remote possibility. . . . the greatest chance of a single event triggering a worldwide financial disaster probably lies in the threat of default on its debt by a Third World or Eastern bloc country." The fifth mentioned crisis is *"a nuclear Armageddon."*

Among the important differences from a past that also faced crises, Neufeld observes that these crises (except #3) are global: "In the past, there was little chance that any disaster would harm all people on earth. . . . today's crises respect no boundaries."

Evangelical Newsletter, 25 May 1984, 2.

Paul said to Timothy, "In the last days there will come times of stress." One of the real evidences of the increased stress of our modern day is the toll it takes on our physical well-being.

ENVIRONMENTAL FACTORS CAUSING STRESS
FOR EXECUTIVES:

Relationships
with superior
with subordinates
with colleagues
inability to delegate
lack of social support

Organizational Structure and Climate
lack of participation
no sense of belonging
poor communications
restrictions on behavior

Extra-organizational Sources
family problems

life crises
financial difficulties
conflicts of personal beliefs and company policy
conflict of work and family
lack of social support

Intrinsic to Job
quantitative overload
qualitative overload
time pressures and deadlines
working conditions
changes at work
keeping up with rapid technological change

Role in the Organization
role ambiguity
role conflict
responsibility of things
responsibility for people
too little responsibility
too little management support
holding a middle management position

Career Development
status incongruity
underpromotion
overpromotion

MANIFESTATIONS OF STRESS
Poor Physical Health
increased pulse rate
high blood pressure
high cholesterol levels
smoking
ulcers
cardiovascular diseases

Poor Mental Health
low motivation
lowered self-esteem
job dissatisfaction
job-related tension
escapist drinking

Organizational Symptoms
low productivity
absenteeism
high staff turnover

Cary L. Cooper and Judi Marshall, *Understanding Executive Stress* (New York: A Petrocelli Book, 1977), 56–57.

By twisting the meaning of words, evil actions become more palatable and contribute to our modern moral decline.

Clearly, a reduction in serious sexual offenses has not been realized through relaxation of pornography laws . . .

There is not only a dismally upward trend in all places where pornography becomes widely available, but the increases show close proximity in time to relaxation of the pornography laws. The possibility that these trends might simply reflect general rises in the rate of violent crime has to be rejected, as I have shown that the growth curves for violent crime reports and for rape reports do not correspond at all well. For example, violent crime in the U.S. rose on average 11% per annum in the period 1960-72 with the rate reducing to 6% per annum in the last three years of that period. Rape showed a 7% annual increase over the same period but, by contrast, accelerated to 23% in the years 1970-72. Pornography is the more strongly implicated in this acceleration when it is known that over the same period three countries that chose to take a firm policy against pornography (Singapore, Japan, and South Africa) experienced no such increase. Indeed Japan achieved a significant reduction in its rape problem. (This is of special interest in the light of an earlier cultural acceptance of rather violent sexual depictions, since it suggests that a curb on violent pornography can lead to a reduction in rape.)

These figures for the various countries are reported in the conventional manner for such data (rate per 100,000 population). A more useful comparison is achieved, however, by assessing the percentage increase from a common starting point and then assess from that point—say 1964. Those places I have studied that gave greater freedom to pornography over the decade showed rises in the rate of reported rape:

United States 139%
England and Wales 94%
Australia 160%
New Zealand 107%
Copenhagen 84%

Those countries that continued restraint on pornography showed a relatively small increase:

Singapore 69%
South Africa 28%

while Japan, exercising a more restrictive policy, actually registered a decrease of 49%.

These recent trends do not allow us to conclude a simple cause-effect relationship; nor can we reject it. They do enable us, however, to challenge the earlier promises of a reduction in sex crimes, and they do also provide a basis for exploring what kind of relationship actually does exist between pornography and rape. "Disinhibitory learning," wherein the observation of specific acts lowers inhibitions against the expression of a wide range of similar behaviors, is probably the psychological mechanism linking the two. Pornography may also serve as an "instigating influence" to rape. This concept suggests that someone with a predisposition to act in a certain way becomes more likely to do so when triggered by a significant stimulus or range of stimuli. It is consistent with the evidence on television violence that pornography should have similar effects.

John H. Court, *Pornography: A Christian Critique* (Downers Grove, Ill.: InterVarsity Press, 1980).

4

Protecting the Homefront

People are always knocking at the front door of your home—the parcel postman, someone needing directions, a young couple taking an opinion survey, your daughter's date. The entrance to your home is a busy place.

There. Someone else is knocking. Now who is it?

You open the door. The man standing there seems familiar; you are immediately drawn to him. "I am looking for a place to stay," he says. "Can I live here for a while?"

Suddenly, like the men on the road to Emmaus, you are flooded with amazed recognition. You feel like the apostle John at a similar appearing of Christ: "When I saw him, I fell at his feet as though dead" (Revelation 1:17). You, too, fall to your knees before your Lord and King.

Does this little drama sound unusual, unbelievable? Do you think it strange that Christ would be interested in living in your cramped apartment, your mortgaged split-level, or even your lavish home? Yet He says, "Here I am! I stand at the door and knock. If anyone hears my voice and opens the door, I will come in and eat with him, and he with me" (Revelation 3:20).

Although these verses are quoted most often in reference to conversion, in their original context they were addressed to the Christian congregation of the church at Laodicea. It is correct to assume that this royal guest hasn't stopped knocking at the homes of church people—He is still

67

extending an invitation for a special kind of fellowship with Him.

So you rise to your feet and welcome the Savior you love who is waiting to enter your front door. "Oh, Your Majesty, please come in. Stay for as long as You like!"

But wait—wait! Aren't there some changes to be made in your home before such an important and holy visitor can start sharing your daily routine? I'm not talking about honoring Him by having the carpets cleaned or the living-room chairs reupholstered. I'm speaking of the changes we make in our lives when we realize that Christ truly lives with us.

Possibly there are items in your house or apartment that would offend Him or that you would be embarrassed for Him to see—certain books, liquor, a few records, posters in the kid's room. What about those things that will detract from the wonder of Him truly being your family guest? The television set? That enormous stack of newspapers and magazines?

What about your habits? If your guest said, "I'd enjoy talking with you tomorrow morning. Do you want to get up a little earlier than usual? Then we'll be all alone." Would you do it? Or would you have an excuse? "I like to read my paper first thing in the morning." "Sorry, but I need to catch up on my sleep—I'll be out late tonight."

Imagine how His visible presence might change the way the members of your family relate to one another. Wouldn't unkind words bring, "*Shh*—Jesus is upstairs. You don't want Him to hear you talking like that, do you?"

When driving home from work I regularly tell myself, "David, how fortunate you are that Christ remains a guest in your home." This has become a healthy reminder. If the King of the Universe was staying with *you*, would you walk into the house and growl, "Where's the mail? Just leave me alone for awhile—I'm tired!" Conscious of His Majesty's presence, would you enter grousing, or would you lovingly ask your children about their day and talk with your wife as you help her put the finishing touches on dinner?

Protecting the Homefront

Although we sense His presence with the eyes of faith, it sometimes helps to recognize His physical presence.

Years ago, we decided as a family to divest our home of anything that might offend our Lord or detract from the wonder of Him truly being our family guest. One of the first things we chose to eliminate was the television set. Television is no more moral or immoral than a radio or magazines, but we found that, for us, the television always seemed to be the center of what went on. It competed with our honored guest for our attention. Many times He had to wait until the television had devoured the better part of our evening. Consequently, all six of us felt it was a good decision when we said, "Let's get rid of the television for the sake of Christ!" That was over twelve years ago, and all of us still feel that that is the way we want it. At various times I have offered to buy the kids sets for their rooms, but they have consistently said no.

Another matter of concern was the newspaper. I really enjoyed my early-morning talks with the King, but I found that reading the morning paper was taking precedence over meeting with the Son of God, who was gracious enough to stay in our home. I'm not opposed to newspapers, but simply to avoid this distraction, I canceled the paper. I even discovered that keeping up on the news without a paper is not hard. And what is more important is that those daily times with my Lord have become richer and richer through the years.

More and more we have tried to make Christ the central figure around whom our family life gravitates. This has made a tremendous difference in both our personal lives and our household.

Do you plan to say no to Christ when He makes His request at the front door? "Live in my life, Jesus, but not my home. After all, a man's home is his castle!"

No! No! Open wide the door of your home to the presence of your King.

Marking His Presence

Throughout the centuries, Christians have depended upon material symbols to remind them of the unseen but holy presence of God. The Jewish people have customarily hung a *mezuzah* on their outer doorpost, obeying the Old Testament directive to "write them [God's commandments] on the doorframes of your houses and on your gates" (Deuteronomy 6:9). The word *mezuzah* actually means doorpost and is a small box containing a parchment with Deuteronomy 6:4-9 and 11:13-21 lettered on the front and the word Shaddai (Almighty) lettered on the back.

In our home, my wife, Karen, has carefully placed the material symbols that remind us of the presence of the Unseen. Her collection of angels surprises the eye here and there. A lithograph of innocent children dancing in a field of flowers before a country church is a reminder of what she feels the Body of Christ should be. Over the fireplace hangs an original painting that a son brought home from Ecuador; its subject is the nations who need to hear of our Lord.

Karen's attitude toward possessions reflects her Christian philosophy. The items we keep around the house are mostly old things that have been used by others and redeemed by refinishing and regluing. They have little value in themselves; their worth is in our use of them. They are pictures to us of the redemptive power of Christ who restores human lives and makes them useful again.

What symbols can you place in your home that will remind you of the presence of your King? A picture of Christ knocking at the door? A Scripture verse framed and hung on a wall? How about needlepointing the invitation extended by the two disciples from Emmaus: "Stay with us, for it is nearly evening; the day is almost over" (Luke 24:29). Whatever you choose, capture a symbol that reminds you of what a glorious privilege is yours to have Christ residing in your home.

Remember, however, that we are dealing with truth. The incarnation of the presence of Christ within our very homes is not some syrupy devotional thought. These symbols, rather, remind us of a truth so basic to our Christian lives that it should overshadow all other considerations.

Along with the symbols, His presence in your home will be marked in another way. You will begin to live your daily life in a different fashion. It doesn't matter if other Christians respond in the same way or alter their habits. Not everyone has consciously opened their door to the King—not everyone has said, "You are welcome to live here." Don't judge others, and don't allow them to intimidate you.

Through the years I have spent much time studying classical spiritual revival. Revival can be experienced by one person, a church, a community, a country, or several nations. One outstanding characteristic of genuine revival is the overwhelming sense of the presence of the Lord.

Revival always affects the home. Families begin to sense strongly the presence of the Lord; they actually experience the presence of the Royal Guest in their home. In fact, revival cannot occur in a church without many homes also being affected. And as long as the special sense of Christ's presence is honored and cherished by God's people, the revival remains. It is that simple.

Protecting the Household

Someone else is knocking at your door. Three young people stand outside—the same ones who tried to sell you flowers at the intersection down the road as you drove home from work. They said the money was for God.

Somewhat cautiously you open the door and ask, "Just what church do the three of you represent—oh, I thought there were three. Anyway, what church do you two belong to?"

They attempt some evasive tactics, but you finally pry out of them, "The Unification Church." Your mind connects that name with Rev. Sun Myung Moon. Graciously but firmly you say that you don't agree with what they represent and therefore have no wish to contribute. You try to get them to speak more precisely about Jesus, and as much as possible, you share that Christ lives in you by His Spirit and that your home is a place where He dwells as your guest. They obviously aren't interested and soon take their flowers and depart.

But you are left with doubts: Did you do it right? Were you too confrontational? Should you have invited them in? Even back in New Testament times people went from city to city, door to door, evangelizing. We know about the travels of the apostles, but one of them, John, also writes that

> many deceivers, who do not acknowledge Jesus Christ as coming in the flesh have gone out into the world. Any such person is the deceiver and the antichrist. . . . If anyone comes to you and does not bring this teaching, do not take him into the house or welcome him. Anyone who welcomes him shares in his wicked work (2 John 7, 10–11).

Feel better about how you handled things? You were in accord with the scriptural mandate: Open the door of your home to your King, but close the door to all antichrists.

You walk back into the living room to tell the family about your visitors and—there is the third member of the group! He's sitting on the couch talking with your children, showing them his literature.

Now you *are* angry. "Get out of here!" you shout. "What did you do, sneak in the back door? You wretched creep— proselytizing my innocent children behind my back. Get out of my house!"

If you think this scenario of deceit and treachery is

absurd, let me tell you—it is exactly what is happening. Antichrist forces have mastered the trick of getting into *our* homes without knocking, and it is not accomplished by sending people door to door. Their devious tactics involve the use of television, radio, newspapers, magazines, books, records, and direct mail—and the recipient is not only deceived but also ends up paying the bill.

I'm not opposed to the communications industry. In fact, my ministry is a media-and-print ministry. But for that very reason, I know just how powerful communication tools can be—for good or for evil.

The alert must be sounded. In too many Christian homes, media voices opposing Christ are allowed to play a dominant role; the delight of the King's presence is no longer experienced or even thought about. Christian parents don't consciously consider what will please Christ most or what will make Him central to their family's life. Instead of Christ, the television set has become the focal point of their daily living.

Have you consciously decided to expose your growing child to 18,000 murders? That's what the average young person will view on television by the time he or she graduates from high school.[1] Your child will have spent approximately 12,000 hours in formal classroom learning but will have watched approximately 22,000 hours of television.

Those figures explain the results of a recent *World Almanac* poll of 2,000 eighth-grade boys in the United States. The poll asked them which people they wanted to be like when they grew up. Their leading role models were, in order, Burt Reynolds, Richard Pryor, Alan Alda, Steve Martin, Robert Redford, and the late John Belushi.[2] Traditional names such as Abraham Lincoln, George Washington, and other noted figures in American history were conspicuously absent from the published list. In fact, no one was named who wasn't an entertainer or a sports figure.

Whom do your children want to emulate and admire? Will they someday say, "Aw, come on!" if you suggest that they should want to be like Jesus?

The average teen will be exposed to over 300,000 commercials in his or her short lifetime. That's over 300,000 messages that, for the most part, stand in marked contrast to the simple lifestyle taught by Christ. Sexual stimulation will dominate what your children watch. Human sexuality is a gift from God, but the media rarely portrays it as He intended. Eight out of ten times when sexual intimacy is shown or suggested on television, it is between people not married to each other. Is that the influence we want in our home and over our children?

Satan carefully and attractively packages his wares. (He, of course, is the spirit behind the rise of antichristism. He *is* the Antichrist, even though the term can be applied to any person or concept bent upon the denigration of our Lord.) He is capable of deceiving not only your children but yourself as well. Unless extreme care is exercised in monitoring your television viewing, particularly with the home-video glut beginning, you may find yourself *enjoying* the very things that embarrassed you when you were once acutely conscious of the King's presence.

If you would throw those bold visiting antichrists out of your home and slam the door behind them, why do you permit them to enter by other means? And if the profanity, vulgarity, and suggestiveness of a Steve Martin or a Richard Pryor (as funny as they might be) do not qualify them as antichrists, certainly they at least merit the application of our Lord's words: "It would be better for him to be thrown into the sea with a millstone tied around his neck than for him to cause one of these little ones to sin" (Luke 17:2).

Again, don't misunderstand me. I am not calling for a new legalism. Frankly, I wouldn't know what to include in a revised list of Christian dos and don'ts—the problem has become so enormously complicated. Nor am I suggesting that Christians remove themselves from the arts. In my opinion, many of our art forms have become degraded because of the lack of the elevating influence of an artistic Christian expression. And I am not advocating a mass withdrawal from the non-Christian culture that surrounds us (if such a thing is even possible).

What I am advocating is that you carefully and prayerfully determine whether or not any evil influences, any antichristism, have sneaked through the door of your home when you weren't looking.

I have concentrated on the medium of television because I see it as the most insidiously powerful influence in most homes. I am also aware that radio is an important instrument used by the spirit of antichrist, especially by beaming music to the younger generation. But it is imperative that we carefully select what we watch, listen to, read, or attend.

While the Mains family does not have a television set, we do attend the theater—both drama and film. For us, this has proven to be an easier area in which to exercise selectivity. Also, Karen and I deliberately seek to expose ourselves and our children to the best our culture has to offer. Each summer we look forward to our yearly trip to the Shakespeare Festival in Stratford, Ontario. Our home is filled with a variety of music, from classical to contemporary Christian. We enjoy a wide range of reading materials, and we continually introduce an analytical element into our family conversations.

An important thing to remember is that we do have a choice, and as believers we must exercise that right. We must get angry and close the door on anything that undermines the truth about Christ. If offensive materials arrive in the mail, write a letter that very day graciously but firmly requesting that your name be removed from their list. If the materials continue to come, write "This material will not be accepted at this address" on the envelope and return it unopened. If a magazine becomes offensive, cancel the subscription. Form a positive defense by looking for the good and applauding it.

The knocking goes on incessantly. Someone is always wanting to enter your home. A few are truly servants of God, but the majority represent the enemy. It is your job to screen who is allowed to enter. In fact, in our time that is one of the most important jobs we have!

Close the door of your home to all antichrists.

Open wide the door of your home to your King.

"To him who overcomes, I will give the right to sit with me on my throne" (Revelation 3:21).

Life Response Section

Initiating Family Lifestyle Changes

Take a walk through the rooms of your home. Imagine that a guest walks beside you through the rooms. This guest is someone you respect very much, someone whom you want to think highly of the way you conduct your life. It is the King, Jesus. Together you walk through the entry hall, through the living areas, the eating areas, the recreation rooms, the bedrooms.

List anything you think needs to be changed—pictures on the wall, books in the bookcases, records or tapes, hobbies that take too much time. Think of both yourself and your family as a whole.

This exercise will help you understand what changes revival initiates in a home where the members are acutely aware of the presence of the King.

Now, take your walk a step further and include family members in this exercise. See what ideas they have about family lifestyle changes that need to be made and that are reflected in the belongings in your home. Discuss any new thoughts this exercise might have stimulated.

Check It Out

Contrasting the General Public and Evangelicals With the Government and Law and Justice Leaders (i.e. Galajl)

	Gallup Poll Gen'l Public**	Gallup Poll Evang's**	Conn. Mutual Gen'l Public***	Conn. Mutual Galajl***
Frequently* Read the Bible	21%	84%	28%	10%
Never Read the Bible	24%	0%	25%	46%
Frequently* Encourage Others to Turn to Religion	21%	47%	23%	6%
Has Made a Personal Commitment to Christ	79%	93%	47%	22%
Frequently* Attend Church	36%	75%	44%	30%
Never Attend Church	22%	0%	18%	24%

*In GALLUP SURVEY used weekly or greater.
**(55 pp. 25–27)
***(53 pp. 215–217)

Protecting the Homefront

Some background on the mezuzah helps us understand how God's people carried out His important commandment that they identify Him with their physical abode. It may also help us in seeing new ways we can symbolize His presence with us.

Mezuzah

The Mezuzah consists of a container of wood, metal, stone, ceramic, or even paper containing a parchment with Deuteronomy 6:4-9 and 11:13-21 lettered on the front, and the word Shaddai (Almighty) lettered on the back. Usually the container has a hole through which the word Shaddai can be seen. Otherwise the container should have the word Shaddai or the letter shin displayed on its front.

History

Originally an abbreviated version of Deuteronomy 6:9 was carved into the doorpost. Later the present twenty-two lines were written on a piece of parchment and fastened to the doorpost. Later it was placed in a hollow reed attached to the doorpost; finally it was placed in a small container.

Significance

There has been disagreement over the actual significance of the mezuzah. Some believed it helped protect their house. At one point kabbalistic symbols and inscriptions were added to further enhance its protective functions. The Shaddai on the back of the parchment is a remnant of this and was an abbreviation for "guardian of the doors of Israel."

A view more prevalent today is that the mezuzah protects the occupants against sinning. Maimonides claimed that the mezuzah reminded Jews, each time they left their home and ventured into the world, that worldly affairs were unimportant.

By the commandment on the mezuzah, man is reminded, when entering or departing, of God's Unity, and is stirred into love for Him. He is awakened from his slumber and from his vain worldly thoughts to the knowledge that nothing endures in eternity like knowledge of the "Rock of the World." This contemplation brings him back to himself and leads him on to the right path.

From *The Jewish Catalog* (Philadelphia: The Jewish Publication Society of America, 1973).

5

The Ezekiel Dilemma

Do you ever wonder how newscasters are able to report grisly and horrifying stories without showing any emotion? Do you ever cringe when an on-the-spot reporter thrusts a microphone into the face of a grieving survivor? The media coverage of the world's tragedies is unbelievably polished, and their casual business-as-usual approach to massacres, holocausts, and genocides seems, at times, as horrible as the atrocities themselves.

Perhaps the journalistic community believes that our daily news is tragic enough without overloading it further. Perhaps they believe that such professional, detached observations are really in the public interest.

Still, I find myself wishing that a voice would crack occasionally, that someone would pause while swallowing back tears, that a well-modulated voice would waver, that someday someone would say, "I'm . . . I'm sorry. I just can't read any more—"

Unfortunately, many ministers fall into the same trap of professionalism. Congregations are no longer comfortable with preachers who are openly intense, perhaps because the media has ridiculed the shouting saints and has stereotyped the red-faced pacer who hollers while jabbing out his points with an index finger. Whether embarrassed by these preachers or put off for other reasons, members of the church have echoed public sentiment by scorning such pulpiteers.

But what if the times are truly desperate? What if they are like those in J. R. R. Tolkien's *Fellowship of the Ring* in which the dark cloud of Morder is slowly moving over Middle Earth? What if evil is spreading its huge tentacles across the nation? How does a minister balance his desire to warn the world of the imminent threat, on one hand, and his fear of being thought an alarmist on the other?

This tension is similar to the prophet Ezekiel's. "There's a saying throughout Israel that I don't like," God said to His servant. "It goes this way. 'The days as they pass just make liars out of the prophets. Unless, of course, the warnings the seers issue are meant for a long time from now. Because (ha ha ha) they're just not coming true.' I will put an end to this proverb," said the Lord God. "It will no longer be heard in Israel. But in your days, O rebellious house, I will speak the word and perform it!"

Yet God placed a heavy burden on His prophet. Ezekiel was ordered to warn both the unrighteous and the righteous:

> The house of Israel is not willing to listen to you because they are not willing to listen to me, for the whole house of Israel is hardened and obstinate. . . . I have made you a watchman for the house of Israel; so hear the word I speak and give them warning from me. When I say to a wicked man, "You will surely die," and you do not warn him or speak out to dissuade him from his evil ways in order to save his life, that wicked man will die for his sin, and I will hold you accountable for his blood. . . . But if you do warn the righteous man not to sin and he does not sin, he will surely live because he took warning, and you [Ezekiel] will have saved yourself. (Ezekiel 3:7, 17–18, 21)

The Ezekiel Dilemma

Talk about being on the horns of a dilemma! The people accused Ezekiel of crying wolf, while God said that if he did not sound a warning, their blood would be on his head!

If God felt this way about His people and the nations and cultures surrounding them, what must He think today about a nation of people who by their actions and attitudes declare, "We are exempt from punishment, harm, or loss. Former absolutes are no longer valid. We can flaunt our nakedness in our movies and magazines. We can display our grossest perversions and profanities in our art and music. We can live in utter self-centeredness and rebellion. Nothing will happen!" A nation of people who respond to warnings of danger and judgment with a shake of the head and a cynical, "Preacher, forget your scare-talk of divine judgment and foreign invaders. Forget about the dangers of venereal disease and the coming of antichrists. We've heard it all before. Fifty years ago men in the pulpit were warning of disaster, and we've come further down the Sodom road. So hush your prophecies, Rev. They won't come true!"

Even the so-called righteous yawn as they become more and more like the world around them. Infidelity and divorce mar Christian marriages. The minds of church children are being warped by drugs and alcohol. Biblical standards for holiness are eroding. The Sabbath is a playground. Christian businessmen are debtors. Justice and mercy are forgotten. Without internal spiritual fiber, Christians are easy prey. Though marked by God as His own, they presume upon His Spirit. They assume there will be no penalty for their wilful actions.

Though many Christians do not want to hear the message, God is saying to His present watchmen, "If the people aren't warned, I'll insist on their blood being on your heads!"

Ministers can no longer be content with mere professionalism. They need a sense of urgency about their message and their ministry, and I am not suggesting an oratorical intensity in the pulpit that simply covers a lack of content.

Quite frankly, most contemporary preaching isn't a matter of life-and-death. It is listenable, helpful, even entertaining at times, but the lack of intensity troubles me greatly.

Ministers, analyze your last sermon. Did your voice crack with the emotional overload you carried, knowing you had to give an accounting to God for your words? Did tears come to your eyes as you prepared the message or as you delivered it? Were you constantly seeking the Lord's approval, or were your motives geared to people seeing *you* and what you represented in a favorable light?

We must continually ask, "If Jesus stood in my pulpit this week, what would He say to my people?" Each church officer and leader, each Sunday-school teacher, and each youth leader must ask, "If the living Lord filled my role this week, would He be as casual about His responsibility as I so often am with mine?"

Our church leaders have become too professional. Like the reporter who yawns in the face of human disaster, their delivery is smooth. But they no longer thunder like John the Baptist or weep like Jeremiah. They have neglected the spiritual power that enables them to legitimately intimidate like Amos or constantly prod people like the apostle Paul.

The leadership of Christ's church needs to bow beneath the weight of the Ezekiel dilemma, caught between a disbelieving nation and a divinely appointed prophetic investiture. They need to pray for this stamp of God on their lives and works:

> Oh, God, help *me*. If I must give an account to You of my presentation, am I in touch with the right topic or am I just mouthing my own thoughts? Am I calling for the response You want? Do my feelings mirror your emotions? Please enlighten me. I am just a human being.
>
> Does sin in my life block You from getting through to me with Your desires? Forgive me!

Oh, God, I need Your help. I know what it is to preach my sermons, sing my songs, run my meetings, teach my lessons. I want to know what it is to have *You* minister through me in all Your power and authority. The day demands it. The enemy goes from victory to victory!

Enflame in me the burning conviction that I am ready to speak Your words in Your stead. Help me to warn the people. O God have mercy! Amen.

Those who pray like this will know what Ezekiel experienced. Probably their hearers will not like the message any more than Old Testament Jews liked the words of the prophets. But the soul of a nation will know that God has spoken.

Reviving the Local Church

Earlier generations of Americans knew something was wrong in their towns when all the church bells unexpectedly began to ring. Maybe a child was lost or the river was rising. In Ezekiel's time the sound of the trumpet signaled distress.

In chapter 33 we read,

Son of man, speak to your countrymen and say to them, "When I bring the sword against a land, and the people of the land choose one of their men and make him their watchman, and he sees the sword coming against the land and blows the trumpet to warn the people, then if any one hears the trumpet but does not take warning and the sword comes and takes his life, his blood will be on his own head. If he had taken warning, he would have saved himself. But if the watchman sees the sword coming and does not blow the trumpet to warn the people and the sword comes and takes the life of one of them, that man will be taken away because of his sin, but I will hold the watchman accountable for his blood."

Son of man, I have made you a watchman for the house of Israel; so hear the word I speak and give them warning from me (Ezekiel 33:1–7).

Ezekiel blew the trumpet and sounded words of sadness and dire warning. Where are the Ezekiels today when once again the people of God face grave danger? Where are the trumpets? Why aren't the church bells ringing out across our land, sounding the alarm and warning about the encroaching danger?

Today believers are under attack from an enemy who personifies the evil of which these earlier conquerors were only a type. The threat is world-wide, but because national histories affect the battle between the spiritual kingdoms, North America is now a critical theater of conflict.

Ezekiel heard grievous news from Jerusalem that was cause for weeping: "The city has fallen." Our news gives equal cause for weeping:

- Our children are being kidnapped for sexual exploitation.
- Physical and mental abuse of women is widespread.
- Teen-geared blood-and-gore slasher films are box-office hits.
- The Supreme Court must rule on whether a small town can use public funds to display a traditional Christmas nativity scene.
- Over 30 percent of all pregnancies in America now end in abortion.
- The *Wall Street Journal* featured a front-page story about prostitutes organizing to fight for their rights saying, "What's illegal isn't necessarily immoral."

While warning about the last days, Paul told the Thessalonian church, "While people are saying, 'Peace and safety,' destruction will come on them suddenly, as labor pains on a pregnant woman, and they will not escape." Then he complimented that church by writing, "But you, brothers, are not in darkness so that this day should surprise you like a thief." Could Paul write those same words to the churches in North America today? Do we live in darkness? Will "that day" surprise us like a thief?

I believe we are living in the days prophesied through-out Scripture. The curtain has opened on the final act, and it is time for the church to begin playing a serious leading role. Earlier I mentioned the need to sense the King's presence in our homes. However, an individualized approach is not enough. It is equally imperative that Christians begin to sense the presence of their Lord in His house, the church. Then the local church becomes the place where God's people become stirred to the realities of antichrist and where they are girded for battle.

When the enemy attacks, there is no time for U.S.O. shows featuring entertainers and pep talks. The troops need the word from the Commander-in-Chief to carry out His orders, to tune into field communications, and to sense that in Him and in His leadership alone there is strength sufficient for the coming conflict.

Specifically, Christians must begin to ask themselves, "If Christ were to begin physically participating in the life of our church next Sunday, how would it change the worship and the lives of people in the congregation?"

Ask yourself that question in regard to these items: How late would you stay out on Saturday night? Would a spirit of anticipation—even delight—begin to manifest itself in your soul as early as Wednesday or Thursday? Would you invite a friend to go with you to church? Would you manage to arrive on time? If you teach Sunday school, would you prepare any differently, knowing that Jesus might attend your class? Would you anticipate any change in the worship service itself? Would you prepare yourself to worship or be content to "sit through it" as usual? What about your running feud with a certain party? Or the way you have conducted business during the past week? Would you have any matters for confession and restitution that you now conveniently overlook?

Such questions, general and specific, could go on indefinitely. But the point is that the church stands in desperate need of revival. Historically, the most outstanding characteristic of genuine revival has been an overwhelming sense of the presence of the Lord! This comes about when *by faith* we begin to act the way we would were we motivated *by the sight* of Him.

If our risen Lord were physically present when we entered the sanctuary next Sunday morning, would we not drop to our knees before Him? Would we not bow our heads and in mind and heart individually and collectively worship Him? Would we not say with great feeling, "There is no other we want to serve"? Would we not express our gratitude at being His people, invited to His house?

When the choir began to sing,

> The Lord is in His holy temple,
> The Lord is in His holy temple,
> Let all the earth keep silence before Him,

would we not respond emphatically, "Yes, may it be so"? Chapter 33 of Ezekiel ends with these words:

> My people come to you, as they usually do, and sit before you to listen to your words, but they do not put them into practice. With their mouths they express devotion, but their hearts are greedy for unjust gain. Indeed, to them you are nothing more than one who sings love songs with a beautiful voice and plays an instrument well, for they hear your words but do not put them into practice. When all this comes true—and it surely will—then they will know that a prophet has been among them (Ezekiel 33:31–33).

88

The Ezekiel Dilemma

It is not enough to sound good, to sing well, to read the text with proper enunciation. What the church needs in these ominous days are prophetic mouths and watchmen in abundance. What the church needs is revival!

Life Response Section

An Imaginary Sunday Exercise

Choose a specific Sunday and do the following exercise. Encourage your family or members of your household to do the same.

Imagine that Christ will be with you *bodily* when you enter the church. What will you do differently on Saturday evening or Sunday morning to prepare to be in His presence? Envision Him in the sanctuary as you worship, as you sing in the choir, as you preach, or as you teach Sunday school. Imagine Him with you as you greet others and participate in the life of the body. What difference will His actual presence make? Will your attitude toward worship or toward others be any different?

At the meal after the morning service, think about what has occurred. Discuss it with family members or friends.

Do you think Christ enjoyed the worship service? Do you think He was disappointed in any way with the morning? Were you ever uncomfortable, knowing He was there? What have you learned from this exercise about your own attitudes toward church and worship? What have you learned about the church itself?

Check It Out

The following is taken from *Revival Lectures* by Charles G. Finney.

The Backslider in Heart

What Backsliding in Heart Is

1. Taking back that consecration to God and His service that constitutes true conversion.

2. The leaving, by a Christian, of his first love.

3. Withdrawing from that state of entire and universal devotion to God, which constitutes true religion, and coming again under the control of a self-pleasing spirit.

4. There may be a backslidden heart, when the forms of religion and obedience to God are maintained. As we know from consciousness that men perform the same, or similar, acts from widely different, and often from opposite, motives, we are certain that men may keep up all the outward *forms* and appearances of religion, when in fact, they are backslidden in heart. No doubt the most intense selfishness often takes on a religious type, and there are many considerations that might lead a backslider in heart to keep up the *forms* while he had lost the power of godliness in his soul.

What Are Evidences of a Backslidden Heart.

1. Manifest formality in religious exercises. A stereotyped, formal way of saying and doing things, that is clearly the result of habit, rather than the outgushing of the religious life. This formality will

91

be emotionless and cold as an iceberg, and will evince a total want of earnestness in the performance of religious duty.

2. A want of religious enjoyment.

3. Religious bondage is another evidence of a backslidden heart. He finds his religious duties a burden to him. He has promised to serve the Lord. He dare not wholly break off from the form of service. The backslider in heart is often like a dutiful but unloving wife. She tries to do her duty to her husband, but fails utterly because she does not love him.

4. An ungoverned temper.

5. A spirit of uncharitableness.

6. A censorious spirit is conclusive evidence of a backslidden heart. This is a spirit of fault-finding, of impugning the motives of others.

7. A want of interest in God's Word.

8. A want of interest in secret prayer.

9. A want of interest in the conversion of souls.

10. A want of interest in missions, missionary work and operations.

11. Loss of interest in benevolent enterprises.

12. Loss of interest in truly spiritual conversation, in the conversation and society of highly spiritual people.

13. Loss of interest in those newly converted.

14. A backslidden heart will further reveal itself in praying almost exclusively for self, and for those friends regarded as parts of self.

15. Pleading for worldly amusements.

16. A self-indulgent spirit is a sure indication of a backslidden heart—a disposition to gratify the appetites and passions of the flesh and mind.

17. A seared conscience.

18. Prevalence of the fear of man.

Charles G. Finney, *Revival Lectures* (Old Tappan, N.J.: Fleming H. Revell, 1979).

The Ezekiel Dilemma

Religion does affect a nation:

In analyzing religion as an independent variable without including marital status, Comstock and Partridge again evaluating the Washington County results, found religion to be protective for arteriosclerotic disease. Arteriosclerotic problems in the cardiovascular system are the leading cause of death and hospitalization in the U.S. Comstock and Partridge demonstrated an almost two times greater risk for mortality for both males and females who attended church on a less than weekly basis comparing them to weekly or greater church attenders.

Finally Zuckerman, Kasl and Ostfeld, in a case control study of an elderly population living around New Haven, Conn., found, like Comstock and Partridge, religion was protective for mortality. In this study marital status along with age, education, income, race, sex, the person's health and previous hospitalizations were all controlled for.

In summary, five separate prospective studies have been presented where both the married and the religious were found to have significantly lower death rates than the non-married and non-religious, respectively. In future work this clarification needs to be made. But both increased religious involvement and being married seems to lower one's risk for dying for males and females. There is some question that marriage is as protective for females as it is for males. There is no question when it comes to religious attendance.

David Larson, Family Research Council. Personal Papers.

6

Unleashing the Power of God

"I have asked people from various parts of the world what they thought about the future," writes Billy Graham in his book *Approaching Hoofbeats: The Four Horsemen of the Apocalypse.* "Most of them hold a pessimistic view. Editorials in the world press are much more gloomy than the American press. Constantly the words armageddon and apocalypse are being used to describe events of the future."[1] Graham, probably the most respected minister of our day, writes this not to frighten his readers, but to urge them to put their ears to the ground to "hear these hoofbeats growing louder by the day."

In another best seller, *People of the Lie,* a book published in New York for the secular market, Dr. M. Scott Peck calls for the development of a psychology of evil. His opening chapter about one of his counselees is titled "The Man Who Made a Pact With the Devil." Dr. Peck confesses that earlier, "in common with 99% of psychiatrists," he did not believe in the devil. Now he does, and because evil is so much a part of the culture, he writes openly and boldly about such matters as group evil, possession, and its cure, exorcism.[2]

Both of these books reveal the intense feelings the authors have about their subjects. Yet neither is intended to frighten readers. Instead, the word *hope* appears at the end of each book.

Evoking hope is exactly my desire, too, in writing about the rise of the religion of antichrist.

Recently my youngest son, twelve-year-old Jeremy, interrupted my broadcast preparations to talk with me. "Dad," he said, "I want to know more about this antichrist." He had picked up snatches of conversations I'd been having with my wife, Karen, as I was working through a radio series on the topic. So Jeremy and I spent time together surveying four chapters in the New Testament. (Whenever my children want to talk about spiritual matters, if at all possible I'll stop what I'm doing and give them time.)

One of his comments particularly caught my attention because it was exactly what I wanted to convey to our listeners about the antichrist. "You know, Dad," he said, "Revelation always scared me before, with all the beasts and stuff. But after talking with you, the frightening thing would be *not* to be a Christian—right?"

"Yes, son," I said. "The fearful thing would be to face times like the present and not know Christ."

My purpose is not to make anyone uneasy about the near future. My purpose is to make the church conscious of the important times in which we live, for I am strongly convicted that I must share the truth that there is a counterforce available to the church in times of great need—in times like this! The power of this force has not been released in our day, but it is, nevertheless, available. It can transform a person, a family, a local church, and eventually, a nation.

This force is the only hope for our land, which is caught in the death-grip of accelerating evil. This force is called revival.

By *revival* I do not mean that colloquialism of our religious subculture that people refer to when they say, "Hey, we're having a revival down at the church this week. Can you come?" I mean the classic, historic moving of God that pours out His presence on a people, a place, a time. I mean the awesome spiritual awakening, like those of the past, that can supernaturally transform small groups,

95

churches, communities, denominations, great urban centers, once haughty nations, and even whole continents.

In a book written almost thirty years ago, *In the Day of Thy Power,* Arthur Wallis paints a vivid picture of what I am describing.

> There was once an ancient reservoir in the hills that supplied a village community with water. It was fed by a mountain stream, and the overflow from the reservoir continued down the streambed to the valley below. There was nothing at all remarkable about this stream. It flowed on its quiet way without even disturbing the boulders that lay in its path or the foot-bridges that crossed it at various points. It seldom overflowed its steep banks, or gave the villagers any trouble. One day, however, some large cracks appeared in one of the walls of the old reservoir, and soon afterwards the wall collapsed, and the waters burst forth down the hillside. They rooted up great trees; they carried along boulders like playthings; they destroyed houses and bridges and all that lay in their path. The streambed could not now contain the volume of water, which therefore flowed over the countryside, even inundating distant dwellings. What had before been ignored or taken for granted now became an object of awe and wonder and fear. From far and near people who in the usual way never went near the stream, hastened to see this great sight.
>
> In picture language this is revival; in fact, it is the sort of picture language that Scripture uses to convey the irresistible power of God. Often in the period just preceding the movement, the stream of power and blessing has been unusually low. The people of God and the word of God have been "in great affliction and reproach," despised or ignored by those around them. In response, however, to the prayers of a burdened remnant God has been quietly heaping the flood. The watchful eye has seen "a cloud as small as a man's hand." The listening ear has caught the sound of abundance of rain. Then suddenly when the majority had no expectation of

it, God opened the windows of heaven and poured out the blessing so that in the channels of organized Christianity there was not room enough to receive it. Like the river that issued from the sanctuary in the vision of Ezekiel (chapter 47), the waters that were at first to the ankles are before long, in the full tide of revival "waters to swim in." The flood of life and blessing has now become an object of awe and wonder. Works of darkness and strongholds of Satan that have long resisted the normal influences of the Spirit are swept away. Stubborn wills that have long withstood the overtures of the gospel, the pleadings and the prayers of loved ones, now bend and break before the irresistible flow of the spirit, to be engulfed themselves and born along in the stream of blessing.[3]

America experienced genuine revivals like this in earlier generations, and we need just such revival today. However, we lack the essential ingredient as a catalyst: a reverential fear of God.

Oh, plenty of Christians have fear. We fear the economic decline, the heated nationalism of the Middle East, the uncontrollable nuclear stockpiling, the evil in our streets; yes, many even fear the Antichrist. But we do not fear the Almighty One, the Creator of all, the Lord of the universe. Yet all our fears, including fear over the rise of antichrist, should be rechanneled into a reverential fear of God.

The New Testament church was alive with the presence of Christ through His Spirit, and the Book of Acts repeatedly cites its hallmark: "And a sense of awe (reverential fear) came upon every soul" (Acts 2:43 AMPLIFIED).

This proper fear of God was greater than the fear of evil, as seen in the incident of Ananias and Sapphira: "When Ananias heard this [the words Peter had spoken about Satan filling the man's heart to lie to the Holy Spirit], he fell down and died. And great fear seized all who heard what had happened." And a little later when Peter asked Sapphira,

"How could you agree to test the spirit of the Lord?" she too fell at his feet and died. And "great fear [here it is again] seized the whole church and all who heard about these events" (Acts 5:5, 9–11).

Later, when Scripture deals with the dreadful coming of Antichrist, fear of God is still the predominant note. In Revelation 14:7, which speaks of the beast and his mark, an angel proclaims with a loud voice to every nation, tribe, tongue, and people, "Fear God and give him glory, because the hour of his judgment has come. Worship him who made the heavens, the earth. . . ." "Fall down before Him," reads the Amplified Bible, "pay Him homage and adoration."

Then another angel warns, "If anyone worships the beast and his image and receives his mark on the forehead or on the hand, he, too, will drink of the wine of God's fury, which has been poured full strength into the cup of his wrath" (Revelation 14:9–10).

Fear can immobilize people. In the past, however, God has taken advantage of this human emotion to push His people toward a greater reliance on Him. Fear of destruction, fear of oppression, fear of natural calamities, fear of uncontrollable wickedness—more than once such fears have prompted God's people to cry out to Him for help.

Old Testament Israel had a terrible time staying close to Jehovah during periods of blessings. Often only desperation forced the Jews to their knees. Even the early church fared better under fire and persecution than it did under favor.

A study of America's religious revivals reveals a similar pattern: First comes widespread hopelessness; then God's people turn to prayer; and finally there is a great awakening. Thus, it seems that no *earnest* cry to God for new life ascends until the old order is gasping for breath. Then fear of the temporal is rechanneled into fear of the eternal God. Hopelessness is transformed into hope.

In 1721 Dr. Increase Mather, a former Harvard president, wrote:

> I am now in my eighty-third year, and having been for
> sixty-five years a preacher of the gospel, I cannot but be
> in the disposition of those ancient men who ... wept
> with a loud voice to see what a change the temple had
> upon it. The children of New England are, or once were,
> the children of godly men ... oh, degenerate New
> England, what art thou come to at this day? How art those
> sins become common in thee that once were not so much
> as heard of in this land?[4]

By 1730 Jonathan Edwards, pastor of the church at
Northampton, Massachusetts, was writing of conditions then
prevalent in his parish and complaining of drunkenness and
licentious living among the youth of the town and of the lack
of parental control and godly example.[5]

Rev. Samuel Blair, speaking of religious conditions in
Pennsylvania, stated, "True religion lay as it were adying
and ready to expire its last breath of life in this part of the
visible church in the spring of 1740."[6]

But there was a hairline crack in the wall. When the first
positive signs of revival were seen, Edwards wrote the
following about his congregation and community:

> Presently upon this, earnest concern about the great
> things of religion and the eternal world became universal
> in all parts of the town, and among persons of all degrees
> and all ages. The noise among the dry bones waxed
> louder and louder. It was a dreadful thing amongst us to
> be out of Christ, in danger every day of dropping into
> hell. All would eagerly lay hold of opportunities for their
> souls, and were wont very often to meet together in
> private houses for religious purposes. Souls did as it were
> come by flocks to Jesus Christ.[7]

This great awakening spread quickly throughout New England and even into the other colonies.

In such special times of spiritual deluge, called revival, the mighty power of the Lord is unleashed in ways never dreamed possible. Individuals, families, and churches are amazingly changed, often at the very moment when it seems most improbable and always because God's people have turned to Him in prayer.

Perhaps the most incredible thing about genuine revival, however, is the impact it has on society. Many people think of revival as a sudden flash-in-the-church-pan that blazes intently only to burn out quickly with little to show for all the commotion. Such folk are ill-informed, as historical accounts verify.

Was the early church a mutual-admiration society, or did it benefit the society within which it existed? Think of what the world was like in New Testament times. Then envision what it must have meant to suddenly find people everywhere who, because they had bowed to Christ, fed the hungry, clothed the naked, ministered to those in prison, treated slaves as brothers, and loved enemies and friends alike. If asked to go one mile, they went two. Their word was as good as an oath, and their lips carried the good news of forgiveness. Of course the world benefited from this truly new society, this kingdom of God made visible on earth.

Did the Wesleyan revivals of the 1700s benefit England? Even non-Christian historians claim that England escaped the kind of bloody revolution that occurred in France because of the widespread influence of the revivals of Wesley, his colleagues, and his followers.[8]

I believe any serious student of past awakenings in America would agree that times of true revival have also been times of true social and national benefit. Whole books have been written on this subject,[9] but a simple testimony may be the most graphic.

The second great awakening occurred in the early 1800s. At that time, frontier states such as Kentucky and Tennessee were centers of lawlessness and iniquity. Conditions were such that a Congressional committee reported on an area of the western territories where only one court had been held in five years. In light of that, note this excerpt from a letter Dr. George Baxter wrote to a colleague:

> On my way I was informed by settlers on the road that the character of Kentucky was entirely changed, and that they were as remarkable for sobriety as they had formerly been for dissoluteness and immorality. And indeed I found Kentucky to all appearances the most moral place I had ever seen. A *religious awe* seemed to pervade the country. Upon the whole, I think that the revival in Kentucky is the most extraordinary that has ever visited the church of Christ.[10]

The moral change Baxter reported had not been stimulated by any government program or legislative act. It began in the winter of 1794 with a group of twenty-three New England clergymen who issued a circular letter that called for a concert of prayer for spiritual awakening. The response of God's people across the land was supportive and enthusiastic, and in about five years "the rain began to fall from heaven." Certainly this letter attests that even raw frontier societies felt the effects of these showers.

Revival will never make a city or nation Christian, since the percentage of the population directly affected by spiritual change seldom approaches a majority. But the number of revived Christians and new converts *is* significant, and the impact of these lives on others is absolutely powerful.

Our society desperately needs another such refreshing visit from God. Although I don't think it is possible to *defeat* the rise of antichrist forces without the appearance of our King, I do believe revival can delay their wicked progress for another generation or two. This delay in itself is a most worthy objective.

Yes, the times are evil, but there is still hope. The Lord still makes good on the promise He gave Paul in the wicked city of Corinth: "Do not be afraid. . . . For I am with you, . . . I have many people in this city" (Acts 18:9–10).

Yes, the spirit of antichrist is real, as John the apostle warned. "Every spirit that does not acknowledge Jesus is not from God. This is the spirit of the antichrist, which you have heard is coming and even now is already in the world" (1 John 4:3). Yet John, too, held before him the eternal hope: "You, dear children, are from God and have overcome them [these agents of antichrist], because the one who is in you is greater than the one who is in the world" (1 John 4:4). To believe otherwise would be to buy into another of the gross lies of the devil.

So if we are living in the last days, facing the incredible evil forecast in Scripture, even that of the emerging deceit-filled leadership of the antichrist, is there not also reason to hope for the greatest outpouring of God's Spirit the continent has ever known? If we are to fear, let us fear Christ and not antichrist. Let us take all apprehension regarding the future and redirect it into reverential awe of our great Lord.

When you hear a troubling news story, don't just shake your head as though nothing can be done. Cry out to God for another revival in this land. Repeat this again and again, day after day, week after week, until the burden becomes an intrinsic part of your life.

Whenever Christ's name is used in vain, speak to your Lord about it: "Forgive us, please, as a people, and hear my petition for another day when Your name will be exalted again in this nation."

Redirect your fear of evil for yourself or your children to hopeful thoughts: "The Antichrist or antichrists, these are only *temporary*. You, Christ, are my ever-present and returning King. Reveal Yourself to us *even now* in power and glory!"

When others express despair, say, "I still have hope! Hope for the ultimate victory of Christ, and hope for another sweeping of His Spirit in revival in our time!"

Unleashing the Power of God

The New Testament church was born in awful days, days when men's hearts were filled with fear. In the midst of this, the apostle Peter reminded believers that their anxiety should be rechanneled into a revived and reverential fear of God and an eternal hope:

> Even if you should suffer for what is right, you are blessed. "Do not fear what they fear; do not be frightened." But in your hearts set apart Christ as Lord. Always be prepared to give an answer to everyone who asks you to give the reason for the hope that you have (1 Peter 3:14–15).

Fear just may be one of God's immediate gifts to His church, forcing us to come to grips with the seriousness of the times in which we live.

May we translate this improper terror into a sustained cry for a mighty break in the dam of our secularized hearts, for spring rains that will wet the drought-seared earth, for flooded rivers from which our parched spirits can drink, for the Living Fountain that never runs dry, for the cloud the size of a man's hand that portends rapidly approaching thunderstorms, for a spiritual irrigation project that will water a continent.

Life Response Section

Building Mental Awareness

Revival is marked by an overwhelming sense of the presence of Christ. Personal revival is stimulated by practicing the presence of Christ in your everyday life, by imagining Christ with you in all that you do. Revival in the home is characterized by a family or a household learning to live as though Jesus were an honored house guest. When there is revival in the church, members act as though the Lord were a dynamic part of the congregation.

What changes would be made in our nation if Christ were the reigning King? List some of them.

Now ask yourself if there is any way you can please Christ by helping to bring about some of these changes right now. Remember, times of genuine revival are always marked by an improvement in society.

Check It Out

Genuine revival always has an effect on society, as indicated in the following discussions.

The Great Awakening and the Early American Colonies

The most significant religious events often appear to be so diffuse and subtle that "hard news" reporters and historians tend to neglect them. To take an example: in the year of the American Bicentennial numerous polls of historians and news reporters ranked the most important events in American history. Never did the First Great Awakening of the 1730s and 1740s show up in the one hundred top selections. Yet scrutiny of colonial life on the part of specialists turns up evidence that this Great Awakening was perhaps the most extensive intercolonial event; that it reached into virtually every kind of community and crossroads; that its effects were at first profoundly unsettling to the established order and then became creative elements in establishing a new order; and that indirect lines connect many of its impulses to those of the War of Independence and nation-building endeavors. Perry Miller and Alan Heimert argue with considerable effect that the awakening began "a new era, not merely of American Protestantism, but in the evolution of the American mind," that it was a watershed, a break with the Middle Ages, a turning point, a "crisis."

William G. McLoughlin, *Revivals, Awakenings and Reform* (Chicago: University of Chicago Press, 1978), viii.

Spiritual Warfare Against Slavery

As is now well known, religious radicals of both Unitarian and evangelical persuasions co-operated to kindle the first blaze of antislavery feeling which swept over the nation. Charles G. Finney probably won as many converts to the cause as William Lloyd Garrison, even though he shunned the role of a political agitator for that of a winner of souls. Among these were Weld, Arthur Tappan, first president of the American Antislavery Society, and Joshua Leavitt, editor first of *The Evangelist* and then of *The Emancipator*. Revivalists like Edward Norris Kirk, Nathaniel S. S. Beman, and Jacob Knapp, together with hundreds of Methodist and New School pastors, lent spiritual support to the movement.

There was nothing mysterious about this alliance. An uncompromising stand against slavery *as a sin* fitted alike the pattern of Methodist perfectionism, New School revivalism, and the intensely ethical concerns of radical Quaker and Unitarian religion. Andrew Jackson's presidency witnessed an immense enlargement of the average man's interest in politics. For the deeply pious, for those awakened in the revivals of 1828–36, such participation required a moral platform. The abolition of slavery was the one most ready to hand. It was, moreover, easily identifiable with their religious traditions. Wesley had called the traffic in human beings the "sum of all villainies." Samuel Hopkins had fearlessly denounced those in his congregation at Newport who profited from it. The spiritual heirs of these two men were the holiness and revival preachers of the nineteenth century.

Revivalists of all persuasions contributed to the goal for which such antislavery editors were striving in the cities of the North. In Newark, Henry Clay Fish cried out in the name both of national liberty and human brotherhood against the slave power. "We are linked together, bone of the same bone, and flesh of the same flesh—the members of one common family," he declared. Francis Wayland told the "Nebraska meeting" in Providence that he valued the union as much as any man. He "would cheerfully sacrifice to it everything but truth and justice and liberty." But, he added, "To form a union for the sake of perpetuating oppression is to make myself an oppressor.... The Union itself becomes to me an accursed thing, if I must first steep it in the tears and blood of those for whom Christ died."

Timothy L. Smith, *Revivalism and Social Reform* (New York: Harper & Row, 1965), 180, 210.

Revivalism and Higher Education

Higher education, developed from the first under the supervision of Presbyterian and Congregationalist ministers, centered increasingly around religion, now that the popular sects undertook a larger role. By 1860 Northern Methodists operated 26 colleges and 116 institutes and academies. Regular Baptist, North and South, maintained 33 colleges and 161 secondary schools. Ministers edited scores of denominational newspapers and magazines whose total circulation had grown to phenomenal proportions by 1860. Strongly religious journals like *Harper's Monthly, Harper's Weekly,* and *The Ladies Repository,* to mention only three under the influence of Methodism, filled a place held later by more secular publications.

Clergymen inspired the dominant social movement of the period, the crusade for humanitarian reform, at every stage. They were the principal arbiters of manners and morals and the most venerated citizens of every community.

The role of educational leaders was all important. Nearly every prominent evangelist gave time and raised money for a college which he hoped would train young ministers to follow in his steps. In this respect Oberlin was only in degree more significant than Amherst, Rensselaer, Rochester, Wittenberg, Connecticut Wesleyan, Ohio Wesleyan, Gettysburg, and Western Reserve colleges and Lane, Yale, Andover, and Union theological seminaries.

Timothy L. Smith, *Revivalism and Social Reform* (New York: Harper & Row, 1965), 36.

The Churches Help the Poor

In a charity sermon which he preached in Boston during the revival of 1842, evangelist Edward Norris Kirk warned that the rise of urban poverty in America posed a new challenge to religion. "Our whole system of education, our modes of life, our very standards of personal piety," declared the newly called pastor of Mt. Vernon Congregational Church, "need great renovation." Instead of shielding their children from the knowledge of suffering, parents must teach them "that the removal of human wretchedness, and the elevation of degraded man is the business of life."

"Infidelity makes a great outcry about its philanthropy," growled the conservative *New York Observer* in 1855, "but religion does the work."

The soul-winning impulse drove Christians into systematic efforts to relieve the miseries of the urban poor. Home mission, Sunday school, tract, and temperance agents early felt the weight of organized evil in the festering slums.

Individual churches soon joined the interdenominational societies in distributing food and clothing, finding employment, resettling children, and providing medical aid for the lowest classes. The revival of 1858 was in many respects the harvest reaped from this gospel seed. It convinced churchmen everywhere that the story of the Good Samaritan was a parable for their times.

Hundreds of city missions existed by 1860, most of them offering temporal ministries far greater than the bowl of stew and occasional night's lodging characteristic in such establishments today. The wartime social services of the United States Christian Commission and the Y.M.C.A. stemmed directly from these roots and were grounded on the same compassion for "lost" men. A large corps of perfectionists flocked to their banners. By the year of Appomattox evangelicals of all persuasions— even Princeton professors—were attacking the abuses of wealth and acknowledging that relief of the impoverished and oppressed was a primary task of the Christian church.

Timothy L. Smith, *Revivalism and Social Reform* (New York: Harper & Row, 1965).

Evangelical Roots of Feminism

Modern revivalism gave birth to the women's rights movement. A recent anthology of *The Feminist Papers* collected by Alice Rossi begins to set the record straight by tracing the roots of American feminism to the revivalism of Charles G. Finney and the reform movements it spawned.

The fact is that the social origins of the women's rights movement in America will not be fully or adequately understood, nor the early feminists rightly appreciated, until the connection is duly acknowledged between the women's movement and left-wing Reformation evangelicalism in America. It is to Rossi's credit that she is one of the first contemporary feminists to identify the connection between the Second Great Awakening, in which Charles Finney himself was moved to support women's right to pray and testify, and the women's rights movement.

In this way Evangelicals began to experiment with new roles for women in the church. Wesley himself gave approval to a few women preachers by the end of his life. And in America the Great Awakenings so reproduced the same phenomena that by the end of the eighteenth century women preachers had begun to appear in such groups as the Free-Will Baptists. Evangelicals did not continue in these practices without testing them against scriptural exegesis, but they found that by approaching the Scriptures with unbiased eyes it became clear that women had played a more significant role in the New Testament church than had previously been assumed, and that a biblical case could be made for giving them more responsibilities in the contemporary church. By the beginning of the nineteenth century new conclusions were being expressed in standard reference works. Adam Clarke's highly influential commentary on the Bible, for example, affirmed of women that "under the blessed spirit of Christianity, they have equal *rights,* equal *privileges,* and equal *blessings,* and let me add, they are equally *useful.*"

Donald W. Dayton, *Discovering an Evangelical Heritage* (New York: Harper & Row Publishers, 1976), 86–88.

7

Change Your Name or Change Your Ways

The pages of history are filled with records of the rise and fall of a succession of empires. In studying them, we note that they all have something in common: Each empire or kingdom or political regime had a golden age, a time when they conquered or occupied some significant portion of their world. Yet despite their glowing military victories and sometimes voracious acquisition of vast territories, none of these empires or kingdoms ever conquered the whole world. Consequently, no one has ever ruled over all the nations at one time.

Scripture reveals that the Antichrist will be the first to do so. Though not all will submit to his will, he will hold political power over this entire planet.

Thus, we must regard the Antichrist as a *world* figure. To concentrate attention on his possible influence on one continent or one hemisphere to the exclusion of the rest of the world is both naive and wrong. Alarm over the acceleration of evil in North America must be put into perspective with catastrophic events in all parts of the globe.

Traditionally, it is preachers who have been accused of rabble-rousing, of manipulating people with prophecies of doom to evoke emotional responses. But today, it is nearly impossible to find a responsible international leader who is saying, "The world is at peace. There are good times ahead. The future is bright. Peace and prosperity for all is within our grasp!"

One day, someone will make those claims, someone with such unusual world-wide charisma that the fantasy of his personality will belie the facts. When this happens, the warning signals should be sounded.

Presently, however, there is cause for grave economic concern. Politically, there is a wild tipping of the balances of power. What leader is not nervous about the need to monitor so many points of world tension? A revival of intense religious fervor fans nationalistic and geographic passions in nations all across the globe, and in the midst of all these aggravations, right at the center of the world, brews the oil-rich, overheated Middle East.

Are we then at the climax, the decisive point, the moment of revelation? Has civilization reached the last rung of the historical ladder?

No one knows the answer to this, of course. Who but a fool would declare that God has privately revealed to him or her His eternal calendar? But then that was the wrong question to ask. All we really need to know is: Do world conditions closely mirror the scriptural predictions for the end times? If the answer is yes, shouldn't Christians adjust their lives accordingly?

What major events need to occur before Christians begin saying to one another, "You know, we could be living in the final days!"

Do we need more wars, five additional nations torn by revolution, two or three new major famine areas, another presidential or papal assassination attempt, further warnings from Alexander Solzhenitsyn, the total collapse of the United Nations? How much more will stimulate urgent discussions among Christians? Or would further cataclysmic events really matter?

Or are we more concerned about trying to move God's timetable along, agonizing over why He delays His coming? Or do we doubt Him because He delays?

"First of all, you must understand," writes Peter, the fisherman-disciple, who walked so many miles with our

112

Lord, "that in the last days scoffers will come, scoffing and following their own evil desires. They will say 'Where is this "coming" he promised? Ever since our fathers died, everything goes on as it has since the beginning of creation.'" The flood came, says Peter; so will the fire. "The Lord is not slow in keeping his promise, as some understand slowness. He is patient with you, not wanting anyone to perish, but everyone to come to repentance" (2 Peter 3:3–4, 9).

We must remember: God is interested in the entire world, not just one country or one continent. God loves the world. His great heart of compassion is still reaching out!

"But the day of the Lord will come like a thief," Peter continues. "The heavens will disappear with a roar; the elements will be destroyed by fire, and the earth and everything in it will be laid bare" (v. 10). There will be a grand finale. For now, though, God waits, unwilling that any should perish.

In a day characterized by the evils of terrorism, sexual perversion, human-rights violations, limited warfare involving chemical weapons, and the possibility of nuclear holocaust, is it foolish to suggest that God holds back the inevitable because in many parts of the world thousands upon thousands are still turning to Him? It appears that this precisely describes God's agenda. According to Peter, aligning our thinking with God's about the end time will result in an even more intent concentration on world evangelism.

For its own sake, North America stands in desperate need of revival. But should the United States succumb to the spreading malignancy that marks her, the ramifications would be staggering! The conflict between the spiritual kingdoms, between light and darkness, is often affected by what happens between nations. Should America fall, for whatever reason, it would affect the proclamation of the gospel world-wide. One after another, smaller nations that come under her technological and financial protection would be closed to the message of Christ. The oppressive political curtains—iron, bamboo, Islamic, and otherwise—would close in rapidly.

I believe we are reading the last chapter of the history book and that there are only four possible individual responses open to us:

1) Yes, we are.

2) No, we're not.

3) I don't know.

4) I don't care.

What is your response?

A careful analysis might clarify whether your response is the proper one for a Christian. Can a Christian really say, "I don't care"? And does "I don't know" seem acceptable in light of the overwhelming evidence of the increasing frequency of the items that make up the catalog of end-time evidences? Doesn't "No, we're not" simply deny the accumulating total of prophetic fulfillments?

That leaves us with "Yes, we are." But many of us are cautious about this response because previous generations felt the same way and were wrong. However just consider the incredible changes the world has undergone in your lifetime.

When I was a boy, we never heard about the possible nuclear destruction of all mankind—even under the heavy cloud of World War II—or of computers that could instantly gain access to information regarding any person anywhere, or of the focus of the world being the Middle East with Israel at the center. Planet earth has changed enormously since those sermons I heard when I was growing up!

For this and the many other reasons I have expressed throughout this book, I believe it is essential that Christians seriously consider the times in which we live. I believe we are already seeing the rise of the religion of antichrist. And if I'm right, the day is far spent; believers must begin to think and act in a manner that is *decidedly Christian* as we face the climax of world history. By that I mean *unmistakably, determinedly, definitely, without second thoughts* Christian.

To begin with, this means we must identify with the concern of our Lord for the lost of the world. As a start, target a country and focus your prayers on it: Honduras, Kenya, Germany, Mexico, India, Japan. Read about current events there and study any available missions materials. Tell God, "I want to identify with Your heart regarding the spread of the Gospel in Indonesia!" Begin to feel God's heart of compassion for that special part of His creation. Discuss your concern with friends and loved ones. Keep a notebook on this land; research its culture and customs; become an expert on it. Travel there if you can. If that's not possible, see a good film on the country. Read books about it. Do whatever you have to do to gain a better understanding of the people who dwell there.

Am I asking too much? I don't think so.

Dr. Harold Lindsell, in his book, *The Gathering Storm*, discusses world events and the return of Christ. He writes of the effect this should have on us:

> Every Christian should think Christianly. There are few Christians who think this way. The Christian mind has become a rare commodity. In many instances it no longer exists.
>
> To think Christianly is to think the way Christ thinks. It is not to conform the mind to the mold of the world but to let Christ become the model for the thought life. We are to think his thoughts after him. Proper thought will lead to proper action and conduct.[1]

How many Christians, now prosperous enough to be world travelers, travel through foreign lands oblivious to the enemy's stunning victories? How many look with Christ's eyes? May God help us change our perspectives. May He teach us to think in a decidedly Christian way.

The fact is, He will teach us. In the most efficient way imaginable, the Holy Spirit tutors Christians. He communicates thought to thought, continually suggesting ideas and prompting feelings.

What if the Holy Spirit whispered to each true believer's heart, "The end is not far off"? What if He conveyed this same message to every Christian in every part of the world at the same time: to the tough construction worker enjoying the completion of a major project in Venezuela; to the Christian computer specialist in Silicon Valley, always anxious for additional information; to the Irish farmer struggling with the high cost of modern machinery? What if suddenly each heard that divine voice in his very soul, saying, "The end is not far off"? Would such knowledge conveyed personally by our Lord have a profound impact? Would Christians change the way they live?

I expect that it would change things in an amazing way.

The U.S. national average of 40 plus hours per week watching television would be lowered overnight because millions of Christians would have more important things to do.

Money allocations would be altered as believers would begin to think in radically different ways regarding investments. Treasures in heaven would quickly take priority over treasures on earth.

A flood of skills and talents given by God to His people would again be made available for kingdom work.

Decisions would be made not on the basis of personal preference or convenience—"I think I would really enjoy that!"—but on an ecclesiastical mindset militantly intent on spiritual warfare.

I envision God's people again thinking in a decidedly Christian way, like the people of the New Testament church. This would bear a marked contrast to present conditions where church men and women think Christian thoughts mainly on Sunday morning or during some crisis or when their youngster asks an urgent question of a spiritual nature.

Change Your Name or Change Your Ways

Old Testament prophets report that God's people of earlier generations had ears to hear but they were deaf; they had eyes to see but they were blind. Despite the authority of His person, Jesus often had trouble capturing committed attention. And finally, God even had His words transcribed in a written communiqué in which He quite specifically detailed the coming of false prophets and false Christs or antichrists, told of great famines and earthquakes, predicted the kingdom message being preached effectively around the world, foretold wickedness multiplying and most men's love growing cold.

He sent His prophets, His Son, and His written Word. Still, people bumble and stumble to their doom.

This inability to hear and see is not accidental. There is a compelling reason for it.

The enemy of Christ's kingdom is a master deceiver. When he gets on a roll, people call darkness light; evil good; killing no more than a woman's personal choice regarding her body. Childish defiance becomes the option of adult entertainment; sin becomes just an alternative lifestyle or freedom from the restrictions of others. And no, this is not a field day for antichristism; it's an enforcement of the constitutional guarantee of separation of church and state. It is for just such accomplished deception that Satan is called the father of lies!

However, God's greatness is in no way threatened by our intentional deafness. God will be God regardless of the fact that the dragon (or the devil in Revelation 12:3) has come to the earth thrashing in great wrath because his time is short. Man's habitual rebellion will not alter one whit what must take place in accord with the Word of the Lord. Even the Bride, His church, who is sometimes uncertain about her love, will not cause our Lord to change the timing of His wedding march. God will still be God.

With that in mind, my prayer is, "Lord, please help me to be all that You desire. In these critical days, help me to be *decidedly Christian,* to be true to what is being whispered again and again in my heart: 'The end is not far off.' I will not wonder whether this message means that the end is this given year or the next or whether it is farther off. I will just accept the importance of this communication and determine that this is a must time for me to think decidedly Christianly. Yes, I hear Your servant Paul whispering from centuries past, 'We must make the most of the time, the days are evil.' "

Perhaps there was a period in history when a volunteer army would have proven effective. Those days are past. The enemy is too strong. All must enlist for this final battle, male and female, young and old. There's an important place for all.

Prayer bands must be formed, pet sins put aside, differences between believers disregarded. God's manual must be studied as never before. Foreign nations must be considered theaters of conflict for our special concern and assistance. Monies must be freed, protest letters written, antichristism challenged, personal evangelism skills sharpened. Specific task forces must rise up in response to the promptings of the Holy Spirit. Pastors must come to the pulpit with the Spirit of God upon them and a fresh word for their people from our Great Commander.

As we conclude, let me again emphasize: *It is not necessary right now that Christians know who the Antichrist will be. But it is imperative that we become actively aware of the current presence of antichrists in our world.*

Beyond people who are antichrist, there is a spirit of antichrist that influences our society. It is important that Christians know how to detect and defeat this spirit especially as it is manifested through the power of the media— television, film, radio, magazines, papers, and recordings. When necessary, we need to close the door of our homes to such intruders. Positively, it is our privilege to open wide the doors of our homes to the delightful presence of our King, to literally sense Him living with us and to make our lifestyles such that He is comfortable with His surroundings.

Beyond the home, the local church must also become a

place where God's people are profoundly stirred by the reality of Christ's presence. As congregations enjoy the participation of Christ's Spirit and prepare for His physical return, they must also be alert to the rise of the religion of antichrist, a true religion headed by an evil, spiritual personality who desires obedience and worship from all.

However, any fear among Christians concerning the rise of this pretender to the throne should be rechanneled into a reverential fear of God and a heightened understanding that the great force of revival is able to temporarily thwart and delay the final elevation of this man of sin.

Finally, the climax of world history is a time for believers to think in a decidedly Christian way!

There is an old story that tells of a young man in the army of Alexander the Great who had disgraced himself by running from the battle. Normally this act of cowardice was punishable by death, but in a magnanimous moment of victory, Alexander listened to the pleas of an officer on behalf of the youth and excused him. The young man prostrated himself in shame and gratitude.

Alexander began to walk away, then turned, and almost as an afterthought, asked the boy his name.

"My name is like yours sir," the youth stammered. "It's Alexander!"

The general was suddenly enraged. He grabbed the young man and yanked him to his feet. "Now hear me," he growled, glaring directly into the youth's eyes. "Either change your ways or change your name!"

The church that bears the name of Christ, the *Christian* church, is in the thick of a battle of cosmic proportions, under the leadership of the Great Commander-in-Chief, who is also our Father. As members of His family and His army, we bear His divine nomenclature, *children of God*.

"My name is Christian," we repeat in safe environments where it will cause us no discomfort.

"My name is Christian," we sing in harmony as we sit eating our church picnics while the battle rages around us.

"My name is Christian," we announce, thinking it an insurance policy against dislocation and suffering.

And God says:

Either change your name or change your ways.

Life Response Section

A Prayer Reminder

After his verses about the antichrist, John writes: "And now, dear children, continue in him [Christ], so that when he appears we may be confident and unashamed before him at his coming" (1 John 2:28).

These are the days, more than ever before, for God's people to be decidedly Christian.

Place copies of this prayer in strategic locations to remind you of the seriousness of these days. Tape a copy to your bathroom mirror; place one in the Bible you normally read; fasten one on your refrigerator; and stick one on the underside of your car visor. Then whenever your eye spots it, remind yourself to whisper this prayer:

> O Lord,
>
> Wake my heart.
>
> Help me to remember to watch for and guard against antichristism.
>
> Teach me how to be *decidedly Christian* in thought, word, and deed.
>
> Amen.

Notes

Chapter One

1. Chaim Potok, *Wanderings* (New York: Alfred A. Knopf, Inc., 1978), xiv.

2. Ibid., 397.

3. *NFD Journal*, March 1984, 5. *NFD Journal* is a monthly publication of the National Federation of Decency, a citizen's organization promoting the biblical ethic of decency in American society with primary emphasis on television. The NFD seeks constructive television programming. Executive Editor: Donald C. Wildmon; Editor: Randall Murphree. Mailing address: P.O. Drawer 2440, Tupelo, MS 38803. Phone: (601) 844-5036.

4. Leo Janus, "Porn Publisher Larry Flynt Beats Drugs But Remains Unashamedly Hooked on Sleaze," *People*, August 1983, 37.

5. William Peterson, *Those Curious New Cults* (New Cannan, Conn.: Keats Publishing Company, 1975), 249.

6. Ibid., 259.

7. Ibid., 254.

8. Bob Larson, *Rock: For Those Who Listen to the Words and Don't Like What They Hear* (Wheaton, Ill.: Tyndale House, 1982), 148.

9. *NFD Journal*, September 1983, 7.

Chapter Two

1. John M. Perkins, *With Justice for All* (Ventura, Cal.: Regal Books, 1981), 165.

2. Linda S. Lichter, S. Robert Lichter, and Stanley Rothman, "Hollywood and America: The Odd Couple," *Public Opinion*, December/January 1983, 1.

3. Franky Schaeffer, *A Time for Anger: The Myth of Neutrality* (Westchester, Ill.: Crossway Books, 1984), 40–41.

4. William S. Banowsky, *It's a Playboy World* (Old Tappan, N.J.: Fleming H. Revell, 1979), 51.

5. Allan Bloom, professor of the Committee on Social Thought at the University of Chicago, in an essay on the current atmosphere in American universities excerpted in *National Review* and the *Wall Street Journal*, May 2, 1983.

Chapter Three

1. James Hefley and Marti Hefley, *By Their Blood* (Milford, Mich.: Mott Media, 1979), 589.

2. Alvin Toffler, *Future Shock* (New York: Random House, 1971), 35.

3. Philip Goldberg, *Executive Health* (New York: McGraw-Hill, 1979), xi.

4. Ibid., 16.

5. Rita Rooney, "Children For Sale," *Reader's Digest*, July 1983, 52–56.

6. Ed Magnuson, "The Ultimate Betrayal," *Time*, September 1983, 21.

7. Ibid.

8. Michael Braun and George Rekers, *The Christian in an Age of Sexual Eclipse* (Wheaton, Ill.: Tyndale House, 1981), 33.

9. *NFD Journal*, 11 March 1984.

Chapter Four

1. Richard L. Fredericks, *Television and the Christian Family Speaker's Manual,* an unpublished manuscript presented in partial fulfillment of the requirements for Course EDRM744, Seminar in Religious Education Curriculum, Andrews University School of Graduate Studies, Winter, 1981, section 1, 7.

2. Ibid.

Notes

Chapter Six

1. Billy Graham, *Approaching Hoofbeats: The Four Horsemen of the Apocalypse* (Waco, Texas: Word Books, 1983), 9.

2. M. Scott Peck, *People of the Lie* (New York: Simon and Schuster, 1983), 182.

3. Arthur Wallis, *In the Day of Thy Power* (Ft. Washington, Penn.: Christian Literature Crusade, 1956), 47.

4. Fred W. Hoffman, *Revival Times in America* (Boston: W. A. Wilde Company, 1956), 42.

5. "A Great Awakening Stirs the Colonies," *America's Great Revivals* (Minneapolis: Dimension Books, 1970), 10.

6. Hoffman, *Revival Times*, 42.

7. "A Great Awakening Stirs the Colonies," 11.

8. Leonard Ravenhill, author of *Revival Praying* in an interview with David Mains on The Chapel of the Air, August, 1983.

9. William G. McLoughlin, *Revivals, Awakenings and Reform: An Essay on Religion and Social Change in America, 1607–1977* (Chicago: University of Chicago Press, 1978). Timothy L. Smith, *Revivalism and Social Reform: American Protestantism on the Eve of the Civil War* (New York: Harper & Row, 1965; originally published by Abingdon Press, 1957). Donald W. Dayton, *Discovering an Evangelical Heritage* (New York: Harper & Row, 1976).

10. J. Edwin Orr, *The Eager Feet: Evangelical Awakenings 1790–1830* (Chicago: Moody Press, 1975), 63. Italics mine.

Chapter Seven

1. Dr. Harold Lindsell, *The Gathering Storm* (Wheaton, Ill.: Tyndale House, 1981).